JULIA BOURN

MEMORY IMPROVEMENT TECHNIQUES FOR STUDENTS

Master Your Mind, Ace Your Exams
(2024 Crash Course)

Copyright © 2024 by JULIA BOURN

All rights reserved. No part of this publication may be reproduced, stored or transmitted in any form or by any means, electronic, mechanical, photocopying, recording, scanning, or otherwise without written permission from the publisher. It is illegal to copy this book, post it to a website, or distribute it by any other means without permission.

First edition

This book was professionally typeset on Reedsy. Find out more at reedsy.com

Contents

1. CHAPTER 1. MEMORY AS A PARTNER FOR A STUDENT ... 1
2. CHAPTER 2: STRUCTURE AND TYPES OF MEMORY ... 15
3. CHAPTER 3: THE POSSIBILITIES OF HUMAN MEMORY ... 33
4. CHAPTER 4. METHODS AND SYSTEMS OF REMEMBERING INFORMATION ... 55
5. CHAPTER 5. SUPER MEMORY TRAINERS ... 79
6. CHAPTER 6. HOW TO USE MNEMONICS IN SCHOOL LESSONS ... 95

1

CHAPTER 1. MEMORY AS A PARTNER FOR A STUDENT

Memory is a crucial skill for students. It has a direct bearing on how well they function at all levels, from elementary school to college. Learning the alphabet, deciphering and committing to memory complex formulas and drawings of Extensive automobile and aircraft models, memories stick with us and serve as stepping stones to further education and employment. From elementary school through university, a student with poor memory suffers.

She struggles to keep up with the other students in the class, which sometimes get her into problems. Most educators and parents do not believe that memory loss is a major problem. They would reject the child, saying that her lack of energy was actually the reason for her poor performance.

The purpose of this chapter is to define memory for you and discuss its significance. It will also describe the indicators of memory impairment so you can look for a workable solution and determine whether these symptoms exist in your memory a resolution to the issue your pupil is having.

What Is Memory?

When we consider the potential of the human brain, it is quite remarkable. The way it operated and the things it could accomplish always captivated me. Just consider how amazing our memory and cognitive abilities are A wealth of knowledge covering a wide variety of subjects. It's an intricate mechanism. The amazing cognitive mechanism of memory aids in our social and personal development. It allows us to save and retrieve specific information that we hear in a college or university lecture. It facilitates information retention and retrieval, particularly during exams.

Our lives are significantly shaped by our memories. It helps us to develop by allowing us to draw lessons from both the past and the present. In general, it is an active, subjective process of thinking back on the past. For instance, you remember the information you hear during a chemistry lecture. It also supplements the information already stored in your brain.

Although memory and learning are closely related concepts that we frequently mix them together, experts distinguish between the two.

Learning is commonly understood to be a process that molds our ideas and perspectives and has a long-lasting impact on our personalities. Our capacity to recall the past is known as memory. Consider Emma, a university student, as an example. Emma is learning Mandarin. She attends the lesson, completes the

lecture, after which she returns home to study the alphabets in a Chinese language handbook she purchased from a local bookshop.

Emma reads the book carefully and commits the lessons to

memory so she can retain them for later. Subsequently, she meets up with her classmates in a park, where she recalls the words and phrases she has learnt. When we are learning something new, memory is crucial. Our ability to store and remember new information helps us to retrieve it when needed. We can define memory as the documentation that remains following a rigorous educational journey.

Learning and memory go hand in hand. In actuality, they depend on one another. Emma links the new information to the information she already has stored in her brain when she attends a new Chinese language lecture regarding the same subject. The learning process is made simple and seamless by this linkage of new information with previously learned information. A university student's learning process will undoubtedly be impacted if they have poor recall. Conversely, a pupil who possesses a strong memory will have an easier time remembering new material. Thus, memory plays a major role in how we learn. Even while memory and learning are related, they should not be confounded. In the human memory, certain processes are constantly in operation.

Encoding Encoding is the first one that comes to mind. Emma's memory processes material from lectures into a certain coded format that is simple to keep in memory.

Storage: Upon completion of the learning process, human memory retains the knowledge in a particular area of the brain.

Retrieving: We are able to retrieve the information we have saved from our memory.

Thus, when we learn anything new, our memory usually goes through three stages. Each of these actions is a component of the typical operational procedure. In general, the effectiveness of learning is determined by how effective our the encoding procedure is. A variety of factors, including the following, influence the active and selective process of encoding:

1. The nature of the material we are studying is the first consideration. In general, it is determined by the amount of information a student is exposed to in class. The larger the amount of information, the more challenging the encoding process becomes. The degree of arrangement of the learning materials has an impact on the content aspect as well. When a student finishes reading a novel or short tale, for instance, she will be able to recall the majority of the material with ease. On the other hand, she will struggle to encode a lot of information in a single session if she is studying anything abstract, like financial data. The degree of familiarity is another element that influences with the material that a pupil is studying. It will be challenging for her to interpret the material if she is unfamiliar with the subject. This explains why first-year students at universities have a hard time during the first few weeks. The organization of the content is another element that influences how new information is encoded. The paragraphs that start, stop, or terminate a piece of material are typically the easiest to encode.
2. The circumstances that affect encoding are related to the second factor. Another name for it is the environmental factor. Although it is typically not as significant as the content component, impacts the way we learn. Environmental elements that affect students' ability to memorize knowledge include the teacher's conduct, the classroom temperature, the amount of noise, the frequency of interruptions, the humidity level, and the student's

residential environment.
3. Subjective component comes in third. They comprise specific components including the student's overall attitude, degree of exhaustion, rest, health, and interest in the subject.

After going through the coding process, the data enters the second step, which is information storage. Additionally, storing is essential to the learning process. We won't be able to do anything if we don't store new information.Think back on it later. With the saved data, there are numerous things we may accomplish. It can help us create connections between new and old knowledge, which simplifies and enjoys the learning process.

Why Do We Forget and What Makes Us Forget?

It is a fact that we often forget even the most basic facts. I concur that a person may find this to be among their most upsetting issues. When they are unable to remember what they have only recently learned, most people become very irritated back then.

We lose track of everything, including people's faces, names, and the circumstances surrounding our meetings. Probably the most frequent thing we forget is our friends' and family members' birthdays. Come on, it's not a big deal if you forget your loved one's birthday. You can make up for it with a lavish celebration and pricey presents. The issue arises when we begin to lose track of crucial business meetings, client names, and the volume of business we conduct with them. Ever wonder why it is that we forget things in the first place? Our brains contain almost a billion neurons, which enable us to perform some incredible tasks like learning many languages and creating things like electric automobiles, robotics, and rockets which can shred the outer atmosphere and take us to space. Really, this is incredible. A person's memory can be so good that they can develop a robot or a rocket, while for others, forgetting things is so common that they need to carry a list of groceries in their pocket (Cherry, 2019).

We frequently forget certain things while recalling every detail pertaining to another. There are specific causes behind our forgetfulness. Let's examine a few of them.

Retrieval of Information

Have you ever felt as though something important simply skipped your mind and caught you off guard? It also occurs with people about whom one may know a certain piece of information but is unable to recollect it or, to put it another way, are unable to locate it in their minds. Their brains continue to feel as though the information is there. Another factor contributing to amnesia is the inability to retrieve a memory.

The decay theory is one explanation for information retrieval failure. According to proponents of this idea, memories have an innate tendency to deteriorate with time. They simply vanish from our memories after a certain amount of time has passed and no one doesn't Get to it. The comparison of a name written on sand in a desert is a good one in this instance. A recollection fades with time, much as a name gradually disappears when sand layers cover it up. The name will remain intact if we continue to clean and rewrite it in the sand.

In a similar vein, if we revisit a memory, it remains active in our minds.

If not, it simply ages like a name in the sand.

However, there are shortcomings to this idea. According to some research, the decay theory is a myth because certain memories stick in our long-term memory for extended periods of time even when we don't practice them. Even though we don't practice them and some of the events from our infancy are useless to us now, we can still recall them up to 25 years or more later.

Role of Interference

The inference hypothesis, which contends that memories compete and obstruct one another, is another important idea. It occurs when the information in two memories is similar. When there is conflict between two memories, they get harder for us to access. Students experience it when they attempt to learn the same lesson over and over again. Let's examine the various forms of interference:

Retroactive interference is the process by which newly learnt information taints our memory of previously learned information.

Proactive interference is the process by which an old memory creates obstacles in the way of a fresh memory being stored in our brain. It makes place for a new recollection all but impossible.

Motivated Forgetfulness

There are moments when we purposefully try to block out recollections of unpleasant or upsetting things that happened to us. Experiences that are painful or traumatic can be extremely unpleasant and problematic for us and might cause severe anxiety and sadness.

We want to move on from these experiences as quickly as possible because of this.

Motivated forgetfulness comes in two flavors: repression and suppression.

Repression is an unconscious kind of forgetting, whereas suppression is a conscious kind. Psychologists typically disagree with repression. The difficulty in determining whether a memory has been repressed or not arises from the nature of repressed memories.

Another school of view contends that the reason we remember things is because we practice them repeatedly and thinking back on them. That's what makes our memory stronger. On the other hand, the least talked about and practiced topics are unpleasant memories or any type of terrible life event. It's the reason we forget them so quickly.

The Storage Problem

Sometimes forgetting has nothing to do with losing information.

It is generally acknowledged that forgetting is related to the fact that certain information is not retained in long-term memory. We in order to store knowledge in long-term memory, our brains must process it.

Our brain cannot convert information into long-term memory if that process is hampered by outside circumstances, such as attentional diversion. (2019, Cherry)

Memory and Mind

The process of stabilizing a memory after it has been acquired is called memory consolidation. Consolidation has an impact on how memories are stored in our brains once they have been processed and stored. various brain regions are engaged in the memory consolidation process. Let's examine them now. **Hippocampal Region: (Fig 1.1)** The brain's process of creating memories heavily relies on the hippocampus. We don't instantly store the knowledge we learn from our surroundings in long-term memory. It is initially retained in the sensory memory before being progressively integrated by information consolidation into the long-term storage.

Since the hippocampal region is essential for the first stages of knowledge consolidation, any harm or injury to this area of the brain impairs our ability to recall specific details.

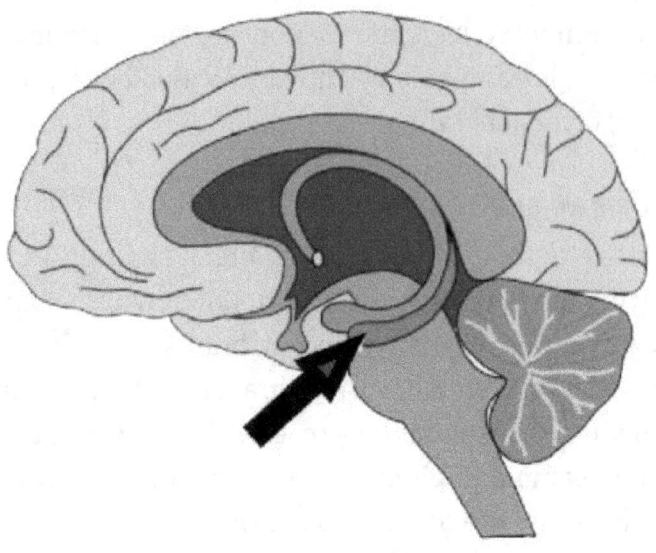

Figure 1

The Brainstem: (F 1.2) This area of the brain plays a significant role in motor learning, including the development of body part coordination. It aids in our memory of how to synchronize our hand and eye movements when shooting at a target during our vacation hunting expeditions. In the same way, a builder learns how to use their eyes and two hands to coordinate when building a wall so that bricks are placed on top of one another. Other everyday tasks like operating a vehicle and preparing food are instances of abilities requiring procedural memory. Therefore, a person's capacity to display motor abilities will suffer if they suffer cerebellar injury.

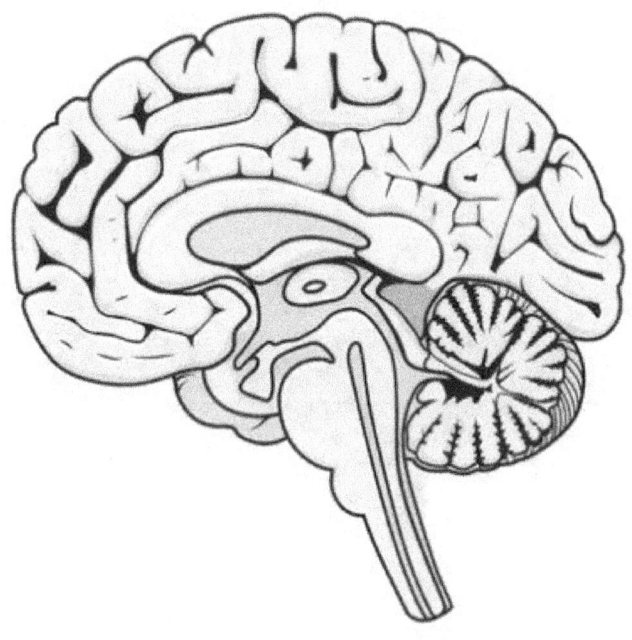

Figure 2

The Amygdala: (F 1.3) The brain region known as the amygdala has a direct role in the consolidation of knowledge within our brains. It modifies the brain's modulation of consolidation. In general, this area of the mind acts as a mediator between our memory and the impacts of emotional arousal. Even in the event of a brain injury, memory encoding is possible. It improves your memory of the specifics of that day, which influences how well you can recall the details of a terrible former experience. Can you remember even the smallest details of the incidents that had a profound impact on your sentiments and emotions, such a distressing abuse episode, a loved one's death, or any other such incident?

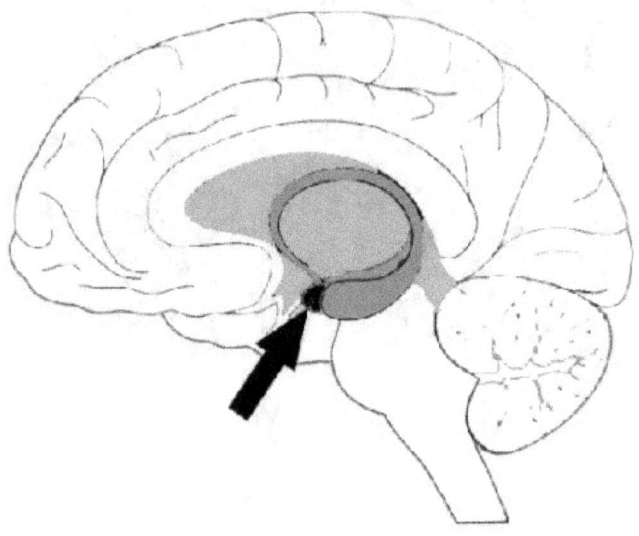

Figure 3

Memory and Health

Who is against eating? Even the hardest people can be softened by french fries served with a cheeseburger and steak. We rarely make a distinction when it comes to eating unless we dislike what is on the dish. It may sound strange, but it's true that our eating habits can have an impact on our memory. It may improve our recall capacity but, at the same time, as we age, it may cause dementia. Green leafy vegetables and nuts are thought to be beneficial for the memory, whereas saturated fats are thought to be detrimental.

Although eating is crucial, how much exercise you fit into

your daily schedule is much more crucial. There are plenty excellent motivations to engage in physical activity. The most well-known of them include reducing the likelihood of having a heart attack, diabetes, or stroke. To lose a few extra pounds, some people work out. Exercise also helps people return to normal blood pressure and reduce depression. Some people exercise only for physical fitness. The majority of us are unaware of the link between exercise and better memory. It preserves our memory and has a good impact on brain function.

There are several ways that exercise affects our brains. It lowers our bodies' levels of inflammation and insulin resistance. It also influences the condition of our brain cells and promotes the development of new blood vessels in the brain. Not to be overlooked is that exercise increases blood circulation in our bodies, which elevates our mood and aids in better sleep.

Research indicates that those who engage in consistent exercise exhibit larger prefrontal and medial cortical volumes, which are responsible for regulating memory activities. Walking is the most popular and effective form of exercise. It causes the heart to beat more quickly, which helps control blood flow to the body's most remote parts. Compared to the body organs below the heart, the brain, which is located above it, typically receives less blood flow.

Not everyone feels like going for a walk. That's alright. Other moderate-intensity exercises that you can do are swimming, dancing, playing badminton or tennis. Sometimes, even doing chores around the house, like mopping the floor and raking the lawn, counts as exercise. Most students enjoy athletics, which is excellent for their memory. You are mistaken if a student avoids sports or any other physical activity, or if you as a parent or teacher believe sports will take time away from their academics.

Participating in sports helps students' memory.

CHAPTER 2: STRUCTURE AND TYPES OF MEMORY

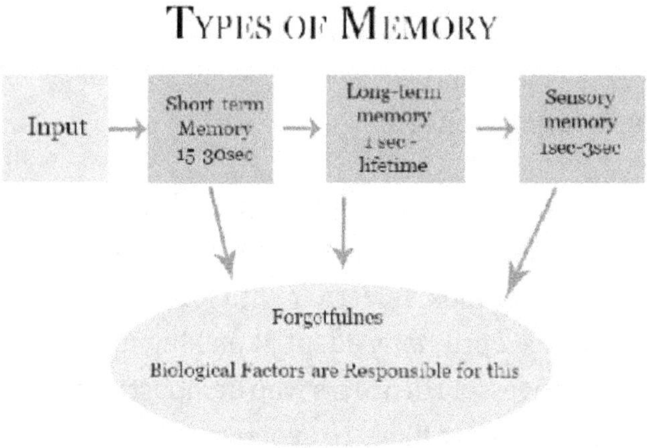

TYPES OF MEMORY

Input → Short term Memory 15-30sec → Long-term memory 1 sec - lifetime → Sensory memory 1sec-3sec

Forgetfulness
Biological Factors are Responsible for this

Figure 2.1

This chapter will guide you through the many types of memory and how our brains use them. Visual, picture, verbal-logic, emotional, sensory, and spontaneous memory are a few of those sorts. We cannot grasp various memory types unless we do not enhance them, nor can we rely on them to enhance the way knowledge is stored in our brains or to increase our memorization skills.

Additionally, you will study motor memory, which is a highly helpful skill while learning how to operate a bike, a boat, or an automobile. Additionally, you will study the various variations of sensory memory. The chapter will explain ways to enhance your memory and also lead you through the symptoms of a poor visual memory.

Visual or Image Memory

According to one definition, visual memory is a quality that students need to excel in any academic setting. It is essential to the learning process for kids. A learner with strong visual memory abilities can be exceptionally adept at picking up new items as well as talks. Conversely, learners who demonstrate inadequate visual memory are more likely to experience disrupted learning in the classroom. Visual memory is widely recognized as a vast domain that encompasses visual perceptive skills. It focuses on an individual's capacity to recollect specific details as they were observed.It is an important consideration while evaluating our writing and reading abilities.

For instance, when a young child picks up a notebook and

a pencil and begins writing a word on it, he or she needs to remember how certain components of the letter that they could recall. In order to write the word "snazzy," he must remember which letter(s) must be repeated and in what pattern the word's five letters are arranged. Imagine how irritated they will be to complete this basic writing task if he has a poor visual recall and the images they produce in his mind tend to go away quickly.

Should a pupil in a student with poor visual memory may find it difficult to keep up with the teacher's marker writing on the whiteboard, which will affect their performance as a whole. Because he will find it difficult to copy the letters from the whiteboard to his notebook, the student will be writing a sentence when the teacher erases it to begin a new one. Additionally, this causes the student to experience psychological problems including worry and an inferiority mentality.

He can have trouble understanding what he reads in reading exercises.

There are two different kinds of visual memory: long-term and short-term.

- **Short-term visual memory:** It is the capacity of a pupil to quickly and accurately recall certain visuals. For instance, a pupil is given twenty brief images to memorize and asked to thirty minutes in length. When the 30-minute deadline closes, they are then urged to recall them right away. This will show how well the pupil's visual memory is. When a pupil copies letters or mathematical formulae from the whiteboard to a notepad, this memory is typically in use.

- **Long-term visual memory:** It is the capacity of a learner to recollect certain locations or pictures that they have seen during a specific window of time in the past. The duration may be one month or one year. A chef The cook may find it difficult to mentor their intern if they have poor visual memory, making it difficult for them to recall specific recipe ingredients. Until a child enters school, where his visual memory skills are constantly tested, visual memory is frequently undetectable. Some parents choose to overlook these issues, accusing the pupils of being lazy and lethargic, but this is typically untrue. You ought to understand what a child is meant to accomplish as well as how a child's memory will impact his academic abilities. This is a summary of the tasks that children who are enrolled in school are affected by visual memory.
- A student's reading comprehension is impacted by their visual memory.

● Students with visual memory are better able to recall words they see written on the whiteboard.

● The capacity to recall symbols on a calculator is impacted by visual memory. ● Visual memory facilitates the formation of mental images of words or letters. Additionally, it assists pupils in making connections between various visuals, such as the image of a horse and the word "horse," so that the learner will automatically associate the word with the image of a horse.

Signs of Poor Visual Memory

Sometimes a pupil with weak visual memory will show one or more symptoms that his parents and teachers need to be aware of. The pupil will display:

- Insufficient ability to retain spelling information.
- He has poor comprehension skills when reading from a book.
- Take more time while replicating something.
- Having trouble using a calculator.
- Slow writing abilities.
- Trouble in recognizing some numbers and letters.

Spatial memory and visual memory are thought to be comparable. It facilitates our recording of the volume of space surrounding us. The way visual memory functions when we are looking at certain items but not at a precise location is where it varies from spatial memory.

Verbal-logic Memory

The term "verbal memory" relates to memory for vocally conveying information, and it is fairly broad. Students that possess this competence are exceptionally productive in both academic and non-academic settings. Our verbal memory is our

the capacity to recall what we read or hear. Verbal memory is very significant since it helps pupils learn in the classroom more effectively. It requires the ability to read, research, and listen. It also requires the ability to remember information when it is most needed. There is a connection between verbal reasoning and verbal memory.

Look for indicators such as poor story or detail recall in order to identify a student who has been experiencing verbal memory problems. Thus, forgetting indicates a poor recall of words. It seems that verbal memory issues are similar to working memory or visual memory issues. Because of this, you should get in touch with the school counselor if you see them during an observation or an objective test.

Additionally, you can take a professional administered verbal memory test (Verbal Memory: The Key to Learning Efficiency, n.d).

There are several techniques you may use to increase the effectiveness of your verbal memory, like dual-coding or speaking aloud while you repeat what you have just read or heard. A useful method for concretely memorizing information is to repeat it aloud.

Word recall and language-based memory are included in verbal memory. This kind of memory is positioned in close proximity to short-term memory due to its capacity to retain information in an active state for a limited amount of time. Three main components make up short-term verbal memory: the ability to store knowledge, the length of time the information remains in the memory, and the encoding process, which is essential for storing information in long-term memory. Encoding is the procedure that makes it possible for you to practice something and then remember it later. (Verbal Memory: The Secret to Effective Learning, n.d.)

Motor Memory

Motor learning and motor memory are related. It is centered on how well our muscular system coordinates. Playing the violin, driving a car, riding a bicycle, or playing other instruments are a few instances of motor learning tennis. If your boy enjoys playing video games, he won't ever forget how to use an Xbox or PlayStation. This kind of precise synchronization is retained in our muscles. Like all forms of memory, motor memory consists of both long and short form components. Verbal short-term memory and short-term motor memory are quite similar. A brief bit of information is stored in short-term memory. Repeating an action several times will help it transfer from short-term memory to long-term memory, which is necessary if we want to retain the process of performing the task for an extended amount of time.

The brain's hippocampal region is where traditional knowledge, sometimes referred to as episodic memory, begins its journey, and the cerebral cortex is where it ends. However, the situation with motor memory is different. Its voyage commences in the cerebral cortex. The purkinje neurons, a particular subtype of neurons, are thought to be the source of short-term memory. Purkinje neurons are in charge of sending messages to the cerebellum, the area of the brain that controls movement (Brown, 2017).

These unique neurons are crucial for because the activities we practice in short-term memory transfer to long-term memory, in the conversion of short-term memory into long-term memory. Long-term memory in motor memory is difficult to attribute to a specific region of the brain. How the impulses from the cerebellar region of our brain affect our coordinated movement is difficult to comprehend and describe. Scholars mention interneurons, which are specialized neurons in the brain that carry impulses to other neurons. Interneurons, according to researchers, provide a blueprint for the movement of specific body parts.

How We Learn to Drive a Car?

A person becomes accustomed to the steering wheel and other components of an automobile when they sit in the driver's seat and become familiar with them. When he initially turns on the engine and operates the vehicle. He is essentially letting his brain process information in small chunks in life. It designates interneurons in the cerebellum to regulate muscle input, rerouting it to the hands and legs to regulate the steering wheel and accelerator, respectively.

Thinking about the process of learning to drive will make you realize that it takes a long time to become proficient and obtain a driver's license. Why do we use so long to acquire knowledge? Like all other memory types, motor memory is unique. It is necessary to practice in order to complete a task effectively. Riding a bicycle is not the same as walking on a pavement.

It takes time for our body and brain to acclimate our motor abilities to the actions needed to operate an automobile. We progressively learn to drive because our body perceives it as a challenge and immediately uses brain cells to acquire this new set of coordination of body parts.

There are many challenges on the first day. Instead of using the brakes, we occasionally press the accelerator. The first and second days essentially don't change. That is likewise how the third day proceeds, however when a week has gone, we notice an enhancement in our coordination of the hands, feet, and eyes.

Our ability to coordinate our bodies more effectively improves with practice, allowing us to drive on highways at top speed without worrying about making a mistake. You'll find that when you learn to drive, you pick up directions more quickly than when you study a theoretical subject. Liken operating a vehicle to carrying out a hands-on experiment in your college lab. Because experiments help learners acquire concepts more quickly than theoretical questions, students adore them.

The process of converting short-term motor memory to long-term motor memory takes less than a week. Even a few days, according to researchers, is a longer period. After just one practice session, we can replicate the identical procedure with professionalism. It is important to note that consolidation of a typical memory takes a whole week. It also sticks in your memory for a very long time. For instance, even if we stop riding or driving for a few months or even years, we still remember how to operate a car or a bicycle. (Brown (2017)

Emotional Memory

Figure 2. 2

We remember some life events more vividly and vividly than others. They seem like they happened yesterday to us. The cause of this incredible phenomena is still something we cannot understand. I mean, there's not technique that enables us to label a particular memory to remain vivid in our minds, but we may almost fully comprehend this unusual phenomenon if we divide our memories into emotional and non-emotional categories. Simply turn back time and reflect for a little while on your present-day memories. It will become apparent to you that certain memories—whether positive or negative—stick out from the others. In the human brain, we can still feel their presence.

CHAPTER 2: STRUCTURE AND TYPES OF MEMORY

The assumption that the human brain has a single memory system was once widely held, but it eventually vanished when it was superseded by the concept that the human memory system can be further split up into several groups. People frequently recall specific incidents from their previous lives, such as a fit of rage or a period of sadness. We typically don't experience the same level of intensity when we think back on a painful experience, like the death of a loved one. But the memory can affect how we feel. A joyful memory can lift our spirits and make us feel good for a while, and remembering a A depressing recollection can temporarily make us feel down. There are various types of emotional memories, including memories of traumatic events like accidents, memories of a loved one passing away, memories of your marriage, memories of your first day of work, and memories of the birth of your first child. These memories are all associated with a variety of feelings, from happiness to grief.

We love to reminisce about wonderful times from the past while we're feeling depressed. It makes us joyful and fulfills our brains. In a similar vein, bad memories can occasionally elicit strong feelings. When reliving the moment when they were mistreated or defrauded, some people become irate. When we consider our coworker who deceived us in order to obtain We begin to feel disgusted and jealous when we are ahead in the competition to land the position of sales executive.

Our memories can just fail us at times. Simple items like the pen we put in our shirts' front pockets escape our memory. We forget other people's names and faces. Among the thousands of recollections, a handful are as clear as an actual photograph. According to research, our brains are primed to retrieve memories that are associated with positive or negative experiences.

A certain due date may occasionally bring back painful memories, such as the day, month, or year when a loved one passed away. I recall meeting a weird girl in a hotel room who professed to be a powerful spiritual person. Her thought process resonated with me because of the way she expressed herself. It has been about twenty years after the incident in my life. Even though I have experienced a lot in the past 20 years, my brain still brings up that specific memory everytime I attend conferences and seminars, and the associated feelings take a while to pass. Because we had met at a capacity building workshop, I can still remember the memory of seeing a conference.

Sensory Memory

People with sensory memory are able to hold onto sensory information even after the stimulus has stopped functioning. It is believed that the brain's sensory memory is the initial step in the memory process. It's the sensory memory that stores a vast quantity of information regarding the setting in which we are working, learning, or sitting. Information is only stored in sensory memory for a very brief period of time. Retaining information for as long as our brain can detect and comprehend it is the fundamental function of sensory memory.

The Working Pattern of Working Memory

We live our entire lives absorbing as much knowledge as we can from the world around us. When we encounter something new, someone, or an environment, all of our senses—tasting, seeing, hearing, smelling, and touching—go into action observe. We have a lot to take in at any one time in our lives, and it is almost hard to process all the information that is being presented to us through all of our senses. We may say that our sensory memory continuously captures images of the environment around us at regular intervals, rather than meticulously recording every detail. We can concentrate on the information that we prefer to retain in our long-term memory out of all these pictures.

The sensory memory is what provides us to see a reenactment of the identical events even in the absence of the initial stimulus for a particular act, allowing us to flip the scene we just saw. We can focus on the knowledge that we believe has some relevance or is more crucial to remember than the others, processing it into our short-term memory for practice. There are various forms of sensory memory, including haptic, echoic, and iconic memory.

Echoic Memory

This kind of memory, often referred to as auditory sensory memory, comprises brief sounds that resemble an echo. Echoic memory is thought to last three to four seconds on average.

Haptic Memory

Tactile memory is another name for haptic memory. This memory stores details about an individual's touch. When we shake hands with new people, our minds begin to tingle with the possibility that we may have met them before prior to. We strain our memory to remember where we first met them. Sometimes,

the feelings are so strong that we cannot restrain ourselves from asking the

person where we met. It is generally acknowledged that haptic memory has a lifespan of about two seconds.

Iconic Memory

Visual sensory memory is another name for iconic memory. Storing fleeting images is mostly dependent on iconic memory function. It is in charge of helping us recall the faces of the people we encounter.

When it comes to taking in information and engaging with our environment, sensory memory is essential. It gathers data from our surroundings by capturing fleeting experiences. Information is occasionally moved to short-term memory, especially when we have a strong interest in it. Large amounts of data cannot be processed and stored in long-term memory due to the short duration of sensory memory.

Spontaneous and Involuntary Memory

There are various kinds of involuntary memories. When we're high, some of them manifest as flashbacks. Generally speaking, these flashbacks are described as spontaneous recurrences based on the medications people take. The frequency and strength of the involuntary memories begin to diminish as soon as the medications' effects start to wear off.

It resembles an obtrusive recall of a previous incident or an unpleasant notion. Our initial response when something like this occurs to us is to attempt to erase the memory from our minds. For a few period, stop and attempt to focus on that bothersome memory; it has something important to tell you. Involuntary memories are thought to become more informative than dreams by experts, and they may may be attempting to convey some unsolved personality developing issues.

When such an intrusion of a memory occurs, you should pay attention, record what has just occurred to you, and think about the connection to determine whether or not it is symbolic of your current situation.

Consider why it is displaying itself at this time. The true cause of a memory's emergence in our brains is something we learn more frequently.

One of the most evident and unambiguous instances are specific recollections that imparted wisdom. One time, for instance, you went to see an ailing neighbor and left your house unlocked for ten minutes. When you came back, your television had been taken. Maybe the recollection was an event when you boarded a bus, it was gone when you got off to get refreshments. When they go to the airport, some people realize that their passport is at home, even though they forgot to bring it with them.

We are profoundly affected by all of these events. These kinds of incidents turn into instructive lessons that stick with us over time of our existence. Although these recollections come at you suddenly, they have a purpose. There are moments when a memory appears for no apparent reason.

Simply said, there is no relationship between the recollection that was just on our minds and the present. You should pay particular attention to this situation.

Certain memories require time to reorganize in your mind. They are hankering after new knowledge to occupy a proper spot in your mind. This type of recollection requires our focus because it gives our lives greater significance.

Semantic Memory

The part of long-term memory known as semantic memory is responsible for processing ideas and concepts that are unrelated to personal experiences. Semantic memory comprises a variety of items, including the names of various colors, the phonemes of various letters, the names and capitals of nations, and any other factual knowledge we are taught during our lifetime.

Although semantic memory was first proposed in 1972, experts still find it relatively new. Two pioneers, Wayne Donaldson from the University of New Brunswick and Endel Tulving from the University of Toronto, were studying how human functioning is affected by organization.

A remembering of facts that we have acquired throughout time since we were young is known as semantic memory. Semantic memory information is not associated with any particular type of emotional or personal experience. Let's examine a few instances of semantic memory.

- We are aware of the following: the ice is white, the grass is green, and the sky is azure.
- We are aware that phones are used to make phone calls. We are aware that the American Civil War occurred in 1861.
- The dog is an animal, as we are aware.
- We are aware that clothing is cut with scissors.
- We are aware that in order to construct a phrase, we must group together several words.
- We are aware that the river runs from north to south, that seeds are necessary for crop growth, and that Washington, D.C., is the capital of the United States of America.

Conversely, episodic memory is highly individualistic. It is the complete opposite of semantic memory and stores various life events and interpersonal interactions that we encounter. As the name implies, episodic memory is made up of various serialized episodes of experiences and events. We are able to rebuild the real event that occurs in our brain by using the experiences and events that we remember. Now let's examine a few instances of episodic memory.

- Remembering your wedding day, your first friendship, and your summertime activities are all examples of memory recall.
- Being able to remember your weekend activities.
- Being able to remember your summertime trips on the frozen lake.
- Being able to remember your very first experiment from

university or college.
- Being able to remember the study tour where you learned about many plants.
- Being able to remember the name of your first pet and your own nickname.
- Being able to name your first cat and dog's breed.
- Being able to remember what you were given for your previous birthday.
- Remembering your very first love.

There is interaction between these two types of memory. Because it depends on episodic memory, semantic memory has a close relationship with it. When we initially discovered the hue of the sky, it was an episodic recollection in which, regarding the hue of the sky, our parents taught us. Subsequently, semantic memory was formed from the same memory. We can claim that memory's permanent location in the brain has shifted.

We store the experiences we have in our life in our semantic memory, recalling certain things as fact. It is possible to state that episodic memory is the source of semantic memory. According to researchers, our brain switches over gradually from episodic memory to semantic memory.

A period of memory reduces sensitivity to certain occurrences in order for it to be recorded as factual information. I had no idea how to utilize my laptop when I first acquired it. I gradually picked up the laptop's tricks. It had eventually been ingrained in my semantic memory. Now I can remember how to use a laptop and its general knowledge. The discussion above does not imply that episodic memories are the source of all semantic memories.

3

CHAPTER 3: THE POSSIBILITIES OF HUMAN MEMORY

This chapter addresses what is possible with human memory. It will examine the controversy about the capacity of the human brain to store knowledge. This chapter continues by outlining the causes of forgetting stuff, so often as soon as we learn them. Additionally, it will clarify the methods that students can use to practice improving their memory and avoid forgetting things. The chapter then goes on to discuss the barriers that inhibit people from learning new things. After that, it will describe the elements that go into the memorization process. You'll discover the negative consequences of an excess of information. There are several arguments that demand consideration, such as how much information is good for you and how much can be fatal for your memory. They are included in this chapter by me.

How Much Information Are You Able to Remember?

There is no set limit to the amount of knowledge our brains can hold, but it is thought to be sufficiently large that anything we desire to learn is independent of our brains' ability to store it. It is able to contain as much knowledge as we would like to store in it, but our capacity to learn is limited by a number of variables. For pupils, paying attention is essential to their process of learning and memorizing. Only a few items can be focused on by students at once. When a teacher uses a book, a whiteboard, and a projector in addition to covering three to four topics in a single lesson, This could cause kids' attention to become fragmented. Making new memories requires a great deal of attention. Here, getting a good night's sleep is crucial since it helps to cement newly formed memories.

If your child attends school, you should ask them to study new material in the afternoon and go to bed early. You'll be astounded by the improvements in her learning capacity that result from it. The sequence in which we acquire different facts also has an impact on our ability to memorize information. For instance, when a child initially begins learning a physics chapter, the first part of the chapter will be simpler to understand and retain than the second part. What we find it challenging to erase what we initially learned. Even when an adult understands that the dark is nothing more than the absence of light, a child's fear of the dark often persists. Any attempt to erase the initial recollection of darkness will fail. Additionally, our brains are susceptible to different kinds of information within particular bounds. At the age of one, infants begin to internalize words and linguistic expressions that they hear from others in their environment. Whatever language they hear, it naturally becomes embedded in their brains. It is known as the "natural language learning mechanism" by experts. As we get older, we have to invest a lot of time in studying a fresh language. Because of this, non-native speakers' accents differ from native speakers' unless they invest a significant amount of time and effort in acquiring the slang and expressions that are used in that language on a daily basis.

Why Do We Forget Things?

When they return home from school, most children have forgotten what they were taught in class. Adults also struggle with forgetting. When we get to the grocery store, the most frequent occurrence of it is forgetting the list of groceries. There is a neurological pattern to forgetting. After a full day or 60 minutes, we occasionally have a blank slate in our minds.

Pupils are adept at editing their work as soon as they understand it. If you observe, your children begin to rush to you to read to you the passages they have just recently remembered. After successfully completing the task, he or she is granted permission to play football because they have fulfilled their studies. Have you ever questioned why your child arrived so quickly and demanded that you hear their lesson right away? It's because, when they learn something new, people are highly adept at recalling knowledge either instantly or after a short period of time.

Another thing to keep in mind is that the child is practicing what they have learnt with this technique. Even if he or she is quick to recite aloud from memory what they have learnt to obtain permission to play, this aids in their long-term memory retention. Even after a short while, they won't be able to recover the material they've studied if they don't do it. Within the first hour of learning a lesson by heart, a child will be able to to remember over half of it, but throughout the course of a day, he or she will forget a sizable chunk of that knowledge. It's likely that every bit of knowledge will be wiped from his head.

The fact that new knowledge in our brains overwrites old information is another important aspect that significantly influences how much information is stored. Another thing that influences it is the amount of information we jam into our minds and then store more of it after we've had a chance to process it. This creates a significant issue and makes us believe that the amount of knowledge our brains can retain is limited.

Can We Work on Our Forgetfulness?

The only way we can break the habit of forgetting and refute the idea that our brains are limited in their ability to retain information is by working on our forgetfulness. By using the keyword strategy, we can increase our brain's storing capacity.

CHAPTER 3: THE POSSIBILITIES OF HUMAN MEMORY

Through the use of this technique, we are able to connect specific bits of information in our brains, thus improving our memory capacity. I am able to associate my buddy Mary's name with the date of her upcoming wedding—December 15th.

Repeating what we have learned and continuing to repeat it for a while after each learning session is the most popular technique for helping us memorize various, frequently abstract, bits of knowledge. You can put your plumber's phone number between his name and the initials of the word "pm." Let us examine the given example, "PL347888989Amy." You can mentally associate the phone number with the word "plumber" in this way.

If not, you'll get lost in the vast amount of data floating around in your brain. Students can be taught using the same example. Students should be taught to make connections between disparate kinds of knowledge. For example, they should learn to recall a frog's organs by associating the words with the pictures of the frog that a teacher shows them during a hands-on experiment.

For this reason, practical study is becoming more and more important in educational institutions everywhere. It makes it possible for students to interact various facts, and ultimately enhances their capacity for remembering. Teaching students to refrain from cramming too much knowledge into their brains is another crucial aspect. We will lose more information if we overload our short-term memory, which is only able to retain a limited quantity of knowledge.

Because practically everyone forgets something every day, researchers continue to debate the true capability of the human brain.

We get really frustrated with it at times. We can only store three or four objects in our working memory, according to several research.

For a short while, our brain maintains information in working memory.

Preventive Factors

The quantity of data we can store in our brains is influenced by a number of different factors. A poor memory is common among those with alcohol or drug addictions. Alcohol disrupts the brain's chemical balance, which causes thiamine to become low. Let's examine a few of the things that keep our memory from performing to its best.

● Should your child display poor learning skills at school, you should go back in time and search for any events that may have had an impact on their brain, such as a head injury, concussion, or bleeding between the brain and skull.

The state of Brian's health is essential to memory function.

● A child whose brain is malfunctioning for any of the aforementioned reasons is likely to be more depressed, unwell, and not very good at memorization. Too many factors, such as strained parent-child connections, a financial crisis, or any other family event like animosity between families, might contribute to brain problems. These kinds of events have an impact on brain function, which has an impact on an individual's memory.

● There is an additional factor that influences our memory

function. Sometimes aberrant protein synthesis or modifications to the hippocampal size also impact the quantity of information that we can recall within a certain time frame.

We occasionally overlook small details, which eventually compromises our memory. We disregard our children's dehydration during the winter and rationalize our inaction by claiming that the seasons have no effect on the fluid balance in our bodies. However, this is untrue. Students run while playing with their friends at school and at home, in contrast to older individuals. That is how they suffer a big loss. water content in their body. Children's low fluid levels have a negative impact on their memory.

- Your child is likely to have a bad memory if you and your spouse are involved in an abusive relationship. An abusive relationship drives your child over the edge and into the depths of stress and depression, which can result in a variety of memory problems in children.
- Malnutrition is another prevalent issue among children. They will have memory loss if their diet is out of balance.

Insufficient levels of thiamine and vitamin B-12 can lead to malnutrition.

If you look around, you'll see that elderly folks frequently lament the poor memory we have. There are various ways in which age affects our memory.

According to many surveys, working memory, commonly referred to as short-term memory, gradually declines as people age. In a similar vein, as we age, our capacity to concentrate in the face of distractions and our rate of information processing also suffer. Like everything else in the world, lots of people continue to have strong memories well into their 80s and beyond. I know a 75-year-old English literature instructor who has an excellent recall of details. He is in the process of memorization more than one hundred thousand English words. He says that eating veggies, in particular, helped him acquire such a strong recall. green, leafy vegetables. As additional research shows a connection between food and memory function, this teacher's assertion appears to have some validity.

- Your child is more likely to become distracted, which could impair memory function, if they are disturbed due to household problems. Our brain is unable to complete the remembering process when we are preoccupied with anything else. Since information only stays in short-term memory for a brief period of time, we cannot store it in our brain if even one step of the memory function loop is missing. We must give our brain time to comprehend the information and store it in long-term memory for storage.

- Lack of sleep also has an impact on how well our memories work. You should have experienced memory loss if you work till late at night on a regular basis. The impact of sleep on memory has been the subject of much discussion in the past. According to experts, the brain's hippocampal region replays and processes information obtained before to sleep before sending it to the neocortex region.

In order for you to be able to retain the knowledge later on, Neocortex examines and processes it. An inability to sleep adequately might cause memories to become lodged in the hippocampal region, leading to problems recalling faces and names. Because of this, experts recommend that students get enough sleep during examination if they wish to score well in the exam.

- Hormonal imbalance is another significant preventive factor that may impact our memory. Our bodies' hormones provide significant signals that may impact how our bodies and brain work, which is why they may have an impact on our memory. Slow thyroid function caused by thyroid problems reduces the amount of hormones that regulate memory. Rarely, it results in dementia.

Weak memory is a common complaint among women throughout the menopause. They gripe about some hazy reasoning. According to experts, a woman is more prone to forget names and tales the more heat flashes she has.

- Certain hormonal abnormalities, such declining testosterone levels with age, also affect men. Studies suggest that hormones related to testosterone might be connected to cognitive alterations including memory loss.
- A young student may experience memory loss if either of their parents or siblings has dementia or Alzheimer's disease. The likelihood of the disease spreading increases if the student has a genetic component.
- There's a positive correlation between activity level and memory impairment. Exercise has a direct impact on memory performance. Additionally, it lowers the chance of dementia.
- Furthermore, smoking tobacco excessively lowers the quantity of oxygen that reaches the brain and enhances memory.
- Another issue that impairs our memory is chronic illness. The flow of oxygen in our bodies is impacted by certain medical problems. A reduced oxygen flow to the brain is linked to heart disease, and this can eventually cause dementia and Alzheimer's (Schwartzbard, MD, n.d).

Factors Contributing to Memorization

Learning anything, whether it be short- or long-term, depends heavily on memory. It is among the most crucial abilities a person possesses. It has a significant effect on our general mental health as well as our personalities and academic achievement in school and college. To put it mildly, memory is not a solitary function. Short-term memory and long-term memory are two examples of the several forms of memory we have already covered. Working memory, sensory memory, verbal and visual memory, as well as spontaneous memory, have also been covered. People from many walks of life come into our lives. Among them are a lot of students. Every kid has a strong point when it comes to recalling information and doing well on tests. A few of them are adept at recalling mathematical formulas, whilst some people have a strong memory for words and their definitions. Some people have an excellent memory for forms, including graphs, charts, and images. Some pupils are limited to remembering only faces and names. They are actually quite good at recalling faces and names.

The several brain regions that are involved in the memory process are already well-known to us. In the brain, every bit of information that is received has a home. We may retain a piece of knowledge in our brain for a longer period of time the more we use it. Other elements that influence remembering include the emotional impact, the applicability of the knowledge we have been given, and the connection to other encoded information in our mind and a great deal more.

We Have to Work on What We Remember

To overcome the forgetting curves, we must carefully craft the information we memorize. A student can review the material if he or she forgets some of what they have learned in class. A teacher could, for instance, present a picture of the bodily parts he needs to teach his pupils. I recall reading in the news about a teacher who showed up to class in a complete body suit with painted bodily parts all over it. He had to educate his pupils about the body's parts that day, so he dressed up and came to the class. Subsequently, he began to literally demonstrate each bodily part on his own body. He said that the method was the most effective way to assist pupils in memorizing information more effectively.

Other methods for helping people remember things include associating the name with an attribute of the individual, like in the case of "Mary always remains merry." "Adam's head resembles a dome" is an additional example. We have connected the names of individuals with their physical characteristics and personalities in both cases. Additionally, we have sought to harmonize physical features with personality traits. The keyword method is a common moniker for this technique. The keyword dome appears in the second case, but joyful appears in the first. The word that is related to them is presented by these keywords. The keywords provide a link between spatial and verbal memory.

Attention to Information

It is imperative that we pay close attention to the information we are getting. It really matters how often a pupil stares at his phone or the walls. He might argue that he is a multitasking expert to their teacher. It is your duty as a teacher to educate the pupils that most memory issues arise not from an inability to retrieve information from our brains but rather from improper encoding. The issue lies in the fact that we never allow the data to enter the system to begin the encoding process.

Different tasks should be assigned to students in order to enhance their encoding skills. For instance, after you have shown them, they should be given the responsibility of sketching the shape of mathematical symbols from memory.

for a bit on the whiteboard. Try using other forms, like the image on a $1 bill or a well-known landmark, to make it more intricate. They will find it difficult to retain a lot of knowledge for the encoding process when you test their cognitive ability. Nevertheless, they will be able to use that information later on. Your pupils will filter out all other distractions when you provide them with a challenge, and this is when the encoding process really gets going.

Deep Processing of Information

You can instruct your students in the skill of deep processing information, which necessitates that the knowledge be related to individual experiences. An English instructor should, for instance, ask pupils to relate certain English words to their own experiences. One can associate light with a sunny beach day. When teaching a noun like the sky, find out from your kids what their thoughts are on gazing up at the sky.

Do they find it amusing or intriguing? You can ask them whether they can relate to the definition of an adjective when you are educating them, like "honest." Try the term "beautiful" instead. A pupil will be able to comprehend adjectives and nouns when he begins to connect with them.

Recall them quickly and effectively. This could be the answer to your long-standing query about why pupils pick up adjectives and proper nouns so quickly.

A learner who has taken a train or an airplane will never forget how to spell and pronounce these two terms. The main argument of the discussion is that knowledge that students can apply to their own situations is more likely to stick in their memory. Sort of like a description list, that is. A teacher's emphasis on reading and understanding will not leave a lasting effect on a student's memory. The whole process that begins when one hears or sees a piece of information is what counts in the information retrieval.

The Importance of Cues

When it comes to memorization, cues are crucial. Teachers occasionally come across a student who asks for a hint or cue to help them remember a lesson from the day before. These cues can be a single term, like the color of the sky, to help you remember a passage from a weather lecture. When professors provide their pupils real-world examples of the principles they are teaching them in class, some students feel more at ease. Examine the following instance: A teacher is attempting to instruct her students on the causes of a tornado's genesis. She imparts to them all of the verbal and visual information about a tornado. However, her students are probably going to forget those specifics.

Asking the pupils to envision some personal recollections, such an episode of an occasion where they saw a tornado, is the appropriate method. Students will be able to relate the terms and their definitions to personal experiences in this way. They will be able to recollect more details about tornadoes because to this exercise.

Be Aware of Information Overdose

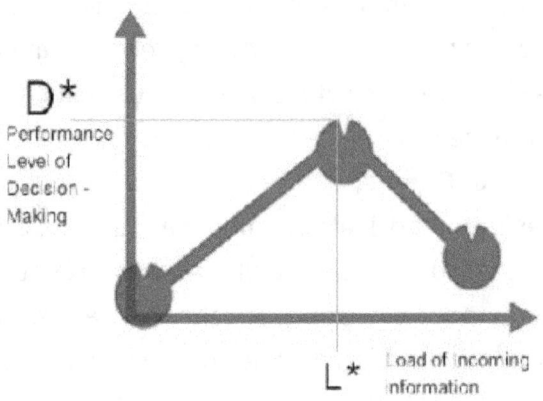

Information Load

Figure 1.3 Information Load

When our brain is overloaded with information, it is referred to as information overload. We are worn out by it. Our minds are incredible. The fact that we have limitless ability to retain information and memorize things is no longer a mystery. The rarest historical occurrences that are irrelevant to the present or the future are the ones we remember. Nevertheless, the intricacy of our nervous system continues to perplex neuroscientists.

Numerous neurologists have noted that although the human brain is able to store an endless amount of knowledge, the constant flow of information in today's digital environment can eventually overwhelm our ability to store knowledge. These days, students use their phones, tablets, and televisions to stay connected to the digital world; this makes their brain overexcited. Our brains experience information overload in this way.

Some people find the idea of information overload to be rather confusing because recent research supports the notion that the human brain is capable of storing all of the planet's information. The human brain's capability for storing information should be more accurately described in terms of petabytes. Scientists surmise that although our brain is incredibly powerful at memorization, an abundance of knowledge might also be detrimental to it. Our capacity to make judgments and be productive can be negatively impacted by having too much information. Students are the ones most impacted by the information overload we are currently experiencing. They have social media and email accounts media, which explains why their email inbox is always overflowing with notifications from various social media platforms, television, and emails. It is almost impossible to avoid the web of information that ensnares students these days.

The human brain processes and stores information from various sources according to a predetermined pattern. We are not allowing our memory process enough time, thus the more information we take in from our environment, the less of it we are able to retain in our brains. Our ability to make decisions has been hampered by this overabundance of information. Employees should avoid having too much information because it may impair their capacity to make judgments.

Consider the position of an office secretary who is responsible for answering emails from clients, shareholders, staff members, and other sources.

He or she will encounter a tonne of material in the form of boss notes and dictation, as well as workspace files in Word, PDF, and Google Doc formats. Their brain's processing channels can become clogged as a result of all much information. The continuous flow of information could start a harmful cycle that eventually could cause further issues for the staff.

Information Overload Can Be a New Challenge

Research has demonstrated that being exposed to a variety of information sources causes the brain to become overstimulated. The neurons that make up the brain are in charge of processing, storing, and retrieving discrete bits of information from memory. These neurons are constantly receiving information, which overloads them with facts, figures, deadlines, and data.

In a short amount of time, a student must complete a lot of tasks, including attending lectures, learning material by heart, reading a lot of books, completing practical work, getting ready for tests and projects, and making PowerPoint presentations. Certain information, like discussing video games or the release of smart watches with pals on social media, is pointless.

When we develop the routine of We are on the verge of damaging our neurons by overloading our brains with unneeded and excessive information.

A stressed brain that is more prone to dementia and other neurodegenerative diseases like Alzheimer's disease is the result of this devastation.

Additionally, by reading publications, news articles, and posts made by their friends on social media, kids run the risk of taking in unrelated information. A pupil has been exposed to the possibility of an informational attack if they are receptive to all of these sources of data. Students experience generalized anxiety as a result of this information explosion, which hinders their capacity to process and assimilate the vast amount of knowledge.

What Are the Symptoms of an Information Overload?

If you begin consuming cheeseburgers three times a day, what would happen? Will you eventually tire of them? What happens if you eat them all year long without growing tired of them? There will be no less of a catastrophe as a result. Thick fat deposits will build up on your back, hips, thighs, neck, and stomach. The same applies to consuming alcohol or any other meal or beverage in excess. Anything used excessively is harmful to humans, if not worse.

Therefore, we may readily digest knowledge if we take it in a moderate way. Not only is an excessive flow of information less likely to be retained in our brains, but it also has the frightening potential to completely ruin our brain's ability to operate. Let's examine the detrimental consequences that information overload has on our brains and our health.

- You will probably feel depressed or rundown.
- You won't be able to concentrate.
- You most likely have eyesight problems.
- You will experience fatigue.
- You will experience insomnia.
- You will constantly be compelled to check your emails, voicemails, applications, and other accounts.
- You'll be less productive.
- Your ability to think clearly will see a decline.

Your child is probably going to perform poorly in school if you see any of the above symptoms (10 Symptoms of knowledge Overload and How It Affects Your Brain & Body, n.d). This is because they are experiencing an overload of knowledge.

Consequences of Information Overload

The American Institute of CPAs and the Chartered Institute of Management Accountants performed a poll in an attempt to establish a connection between decision-making abilities and an abundance of information. The purpose of the poll was to investigate the reasons behind certain senior executives' difficulties in making decisions. A study on CEOs from a few high-level firms from about 16 different nations was included in this survey.

"The prevailing belief in the era of big data has been that the more, the better. However, our research indicates that big data actually makes decision-makers' lives more difficult in many firms because it makes it difficult for them to extract pertinent information and transform it into insight. Possessing an in-depth comprehension of the nonfinancial and financial value drivers Barry Melancon, CPA, CGMA, President and CEO of the American Institute of Certified Public Accountants (AICPA), stated that the accounting and finance function of the business is essential to achieving a competitive advantage for business (Tilley and Melancon, 2016).

According to the survey, about sixteen percent of executives claimed that their company was unable to figure out how to handle information overload. The survey also revealed that employees will experience stress and anxiety as a result of an information overload. Overwhelming information might cause employees to become disengaged and less productive.

What Can Be Done to Avoid the Information Overload?

People and objects generally pique the curiosity of humans. They get bored with old and worn-out information, thus they are constantly eager for new information. We are becoming more inquisitive and insatiable in today's environment since we can always get new information, no matter where we are. We are only a few keystrokes away from anything. We can glance over as many resources as we like on Google whenever a query occurs to us. While ingesting vast amounts of information is perfectly acceptable, we must exercise caution in selecting the methods that will most effectively restore normal brain function.

Below is a summary of some methods to normalize the

function of your brain.

Be choosy with respect to information sources: As humans, we enjoy hearing many viewpoints from a variety of information sources, but not all of these sources can be trusted. This results in a deluge of misleading information that may have detrimental effects on our brains. The only way to address this problem is to teach students' brains to check the accuracy of information before allowing it to enter their system.

Install an information filter in the brain: Students today are surrounded by a sea of knowledge that comes from a variety of sources, including the internet and classrooms. It is important to teach pupils how to sift through material and only consider absorbing that which adds value to their existing knowledge. It implies that students ought to weed out gossip from talk shows and unrelated stories, like the story of a cat being saved from a snow-covered lawn. These items don't matter and only serve to further perplex the minds of the pupils (10 Symptoms of Information Overload and How It Affects Your Brain & Body, n.d).

Refuse to do things that drain you out: Say "no" to activities that take up all of your energy, such as completing actual job or quickly scanning through newspapers to learn about the stock market. The efficiency and caliber of your brain's performance will decrease if you are taking in information that makes your brain feel more tired. It will therefore have an impact on the outcomes you anticipate.

Choose whom to talk to: People's dispositions vary. While some people enjoy talking slowly, others enjoy talking excessively. Some of them will jam as many unimportant facts as possible into their small conversation. Many people enjoy having numerous conversations at once in an attempt to make sense of it all. It is important to teach students how to discern who to talk to and who to avoid. Some people are emotionally draining and mentally taxing, some talk excessively, and some people enjoy confiding in us about their personal issues. Before spending time with someone, we should instill in our kids the value of forming an opinion on them.

Students should set limits: Students must be taught to place boundaries on the flow of information. Getting in touch with the newspaper during breakfast is not required. Creating and posting a post on Facebook, Instagram, or Twitter is also not required. You have a few days to put social media on snooze. To break up the monotony of their daily schedule, students should be taught to ignore using social media, reading newspapers and periodicals, and engaging in gossip. They won't become dependent on consuming information after the consistency is broken. They ought to understand that it is not their responsibility to constantly bombard their minds with knowledge that will rarely benefit them. They ought to be taught to impose daily restrictions on how many times they read the newspaper or post on social media. If it isn't possible, a daily time limit can be imposed on how much time they spend on these activities. For instance, a student may designate ten minutes as their allotment for social media browsing or newspaper reading (10 Signs of Information Overload and How It Affects Your Brain & Body, n.d.).

You should prioritize your activities: Certain activities are more significant than others. Avoid packing your schedule with too many things that demand all of your attention. A student needs to watch their favorite TV show, learn the things they are taught in class by heart, and keep up with current events. They ought to order the incoming information according to what is most important to them. Their main focus should be on the lessons they learned in school. In a similar vein, other items ought to be placed in the order of their choosing. By doing this, he or she can train their brain to process the information they find most interesting and filter out the irrelevant stuff. This is an excellent method to avoid information overload (10 Signs of Information Overload and How It Impacts Both Your Body and Brain, n.d.).

Do what you think is right: A student cannot effectively meet all of their obligations if they take it upon themselves to handle their coursework, athletics, and extracurricular activities. An excessive amount of responsibility can negatively impact their brain. It causes young people to become overstimulated, which raises their risk of stroke. For this reason, teaching pupils how to unwind is a good idea. Parents' expectations can sometimes cause a student to become even more exhausted, leading them to start working longer hours than is healthy in order to meet their expectations. Experts claim that plenty of outdoor activities like swimming, hunting, and other outdoor pursuits, together with physical activity, restful sleep, and regular hydration, can truly assist regulate this kind of concerning condition. Teachers and parents can each have a part in Including these activities in students' daily lives.

Spend time alone: It is important to teach students how to take short breaks for comfort. To be in a state of solace, one should not be distracted by sounds, the internet, or other people. They ought to give themselves a break to organize their thoughts and deal with anything that is really bothering them. You will be better able to filter the information you are getting and make decisions about what to accept or reject after spending time by yourself. It is also beneficial for setting priorities (10 Signs of

Information Overload and How It Impacts Your Body & Brain, n.d.).

4

CHAPTER 4. METHODS AND SYSTEMS OF REMEMBERING INFORMATION

This chapter includes a thorough section on outlining the fundamental concepts of information retention, including student interest, the value of recitation, the significance of association, the organization of ideas in our minds, prior knowledge of the subjects you are trying to memorize, and the consolidation of information.

The section that follows provides details on a variety of strategies for helping you retain information. You can identify memory locations, stack the information blocks, transform the material into visuals, and modify your study habits. To help you recall things better, you should begin studying in the afternoon.

The chapter's third portion will go into how emotions affect our memory. It will guide you through the significance of emotional content, our emotional condition, and the relationship between attention and emotions. The significance of attention and how it relates to memory are discussed in the chapter's last part. You will understand the significance of paying close attention to the information you wish to permanently implant in your brain. At the end of the chapter is a remark about imagination and the text verbatim.

Basic Principles of Remembering

When we are learning something, there are several information-memorization guidelines that are important to follow. Certain ones are too simple for students to learn anything at all. Without the right instruction, it is impossible to expect a pupil to acquire memorization well because it is a complex process. Here is a summary of the key ideas that students should keep in mind in order to efficiently memorize information.

The Interest Factor

A student who has buckled under parental pressure and chosen medicine over software engineering will continue to struggle with memorization because she won't be able to demonstrate the same level of interest in the subject matter as she might have for the software engineering lessons. You have to first cultivate interest in the subject if you want to retain it effectively and thoroughly. The majority of the time, pupils' inability to memorize even basic information is caused by their disinterest in the material. There should be a purpose for students to learn what is expected of them. When a student gets bored in class, there are a few strategies they can use to keep themselves engaged. A student can locate a study companion who will keep them company both at home and during class. To make your child feel comfortable in class, as a parent, you can assist them in developing a cordial relationship with their lecturer. To achieve better in class, teachers might motivate their students to practice and research more.

You may get him or her a new tablet or laptop so they can do medical research. You can also purchase fresh herbs and plants for them, which will benefit their academic endeavors.

During a live presentation or group study, students ought to be motivated to impart their knowledge to other students. Students ought to be encouraged to participate in the practical domain by applying the knowledge they have learned in the classroom to real-world activities.

Students Should Have the Intention to Remember

When it comes to memorization, intention and attention are strongly related. Things matter more than what we have on our plates, depending on how willing we are to recall them.

Simply put, students don't focus on what they are reading.

Every time they pick up a book or a copy of their notes, they frequently battle with straying thoughts. When they are in class, their minds begin to wander to their PlayStations or friends. This is because they let their brain to graze on their favorite memory during the lecture because they don't attempt to memorize anything.

In order to retain the information they read in their books and hear from their professors, students need use focus and concentration strategies. You won't be able to overcome this issue and improve your long-term memory without paying close attention. It is important to prepare students for quizzes that follow lectures. They will learn attentively in this method. After every session, they can also be asked to anticipate a reward. They may also be handed a concentration check sheet, which they are to use as a reminder to keep oneself focused if they catch themselves not paying attention. Students will be able to better prepare their brains to memorize information in this way.

Asking lots of questions throughout the presentation is another crucial thing to think about. If a student is unclear about anything related to the current topic, teachers should encourage them to ask questions. Teachers can interact with students by asking them what they have learned so far and how they can apply that material to their everyday life, even if they are hesitant or don't want to ask questions. For instance, when a medical student is studying eucalyptus and its use in the creation of various medications, the instructor may quiz the student on the plant's appearance and how frequently they have seen it in person or on the internet.

Background Knowledge of Things Really Matters

When a student is familiar with a subject they are studying in school, they will pick up new information about it more rapidly.

Prior knowledge has a beneficial impact on how well new information on the same topic is absorbed and retained. For instance, a student who enjoys gardening and trees has previously planted a drove in her backyard for entertainment purposes. She'll be able to do exceptionally well in school if she understands the functions of plants and trees. Thus, having a foundational understanding of things is essential. If a student doesn't understand the fundamentals, such how computers operate and what apps must be installed on the system in order to make It is ready for coding in its entirety. The best course of action if you want your child to pursue a career in artificial intelligence after graduation is to get a decent computer and a few inexpensive robots. This will assist them in understanding artificial intelligence, including its definition, mechanisms, and global applications.

Your child can learn more about artificial intelligence by conducting more online research. Taking them on a guest visit to Tesla's headquarters to demonstrate how artificial intelligence is sweeping the globe is a smart idea. Additionally, individuals can first finish a few foundational courses to familiarize themselves with the method via which the systems function.

Organization of Ideas Matters

Random thought processing is not a strong suit for our brain. We will recall knowledge more effectively if it is presented as a collection of concepts packaged into meaningful packets. According to experts, a person can only recall seven things at once. It should be taught to students to synthesize vast amounts of knowledge that have personal significance. The plants that are utilized to manufacture medicines for disorders of the nervous system can be grouped by our medical student. It might contain a little amount of alcohol and an opium extract, which are typically added to medications to aid in sedation. The group of plants consists of grapes, sugarcane, and opium. These are all utilized to produce extracts that aid in promoting sleep among patients.

In a similar vein, students studying English literature can organize a group of romantic writers. Arranging vegetables according to size, color, or flavor in a group will help students learn the names of the vegetables by heart. Thus, it's also an enjoyable exercise. A history student can draw connections between the reigns of various monarchs by considering their preferences. In an English language class, a student can select a list of adjectives and relate them to characteristics of a person or of oneself. They can learn quickly and effectively in this way.

Based on the facts that have personal significance for them, a student can classify a collection of items in a individual level. If the person like milk, they will have no trouble remembering the names of all raw and value-added milk-related foods, including butter, yogurt, and pasteurized milk.

Mnemonics are a useful method for helping people memorize word and phrase groups. I'll walk you through the process of making and using mnemonics in great detail. For now, know that mnemonics assist you in creating words by combining the initial letter of each word to create a word that is easy for you to recall.

Recitation of What You Learn at School

It's important for students to get into the practice of saying aloud everything they learn in class. For moving information from our short-term memory to our long-term memory, this is one of the most effective tools we have.

Teachers frequently assign pupils to recite tables, alphabets, and numerals aloud since they, the majority of them, are fully

CHAPTER 4. METHODS AND SYSTEMS OF REMEMBERING INFORMATION

aware of the method's usefulness. When learning a subject, students ought to be encouraged to use this kind of approach at home as well. The ideal setting for this exercise is probably a room by yourself.

First off, the science behind this type of instruction is that when students are speaking out and using their own words, they are more likely to pay attention to the lesson. Second, you can receive immediate feedback on the knowledge you have acquired. You can understand something better when you are saying it loudly enough for yourself to hear. You may say that you are retraining yourself. Thirdly, you have access to several brain regions.

A learner can hear material through their ears, which triggers a separate area of their brain, when they recite a lesson aloud. Everything they hear is absorbed into the short-term memory, where the brain practices it before storing it in the long-term memory. Recitation increases the likelihood that the information will be practiced and consolidated in long-term memory (Memory Principles, n.d.).

You can use a book, a journal, or a flashcard for this exercise. Read the paragraph aloud to yourself first, then repeat it. Do this exercise a few times over. If you find this difficult, you can ask a classmate to visit you at home and lead you through the activity while providing food.

Association of Information

This is yet another effective strategy for long-term memorization.

Our brain's intrinsic wiring allows it to process new information rapidly if it can establish a connection with previously stored knowledge. Our brain is able to construct a chain in this way. Memorization is made easy when we can recall previously learned material and make connections between new and existing information stored in the brain. Students can use the same approach.

A teacher should ask a student to locate any prior knowledge in their brain that might be related to the new material they have learned. The pupil have to ask oneself if they are capable of fishing out something from their stored mental information. They are able to link the sound of new information to historical data. Our minds function similarly to a warehouse. We have many cabinets and files where we have kept various bits of information. Our brain works to establish a new file, cabinet, or drawer where it may store new knowledge when it becomes available. The brain's storage becomes completely unfamiliar with the memory. Because rehearsal gets rid of the weirdness, we can remember things for longer when we practice them.

What happens if the pupil is able to connect a piece of knowledge from the storeroom with the new information? Our brain will gather the data. and process it to the particular file or cabinet that has an old memory (Memory Principles, n.d).

It's possible that the pupil we've been discussing saw the pine tree while on a parental vacation in the great outdoors. The pine tree's memory is stored in the brain for the previous 24 months. The pupil is now enrolled in class. They instantly recall the previous piece of knowledge and make the connection when their teacher describes the name, shape, and various features of the pine tree. In this way, the new knowledge can be reinforced by the old memory and stored more quickly than it would otherwise.

By establishing a rational connection between various facts, we can strengthen our capacity for learning and memorizing.

Consolidation of Information

CHAPTER 4. METHODS AND SYSTEMS OF REMEMBERING INFORMATION

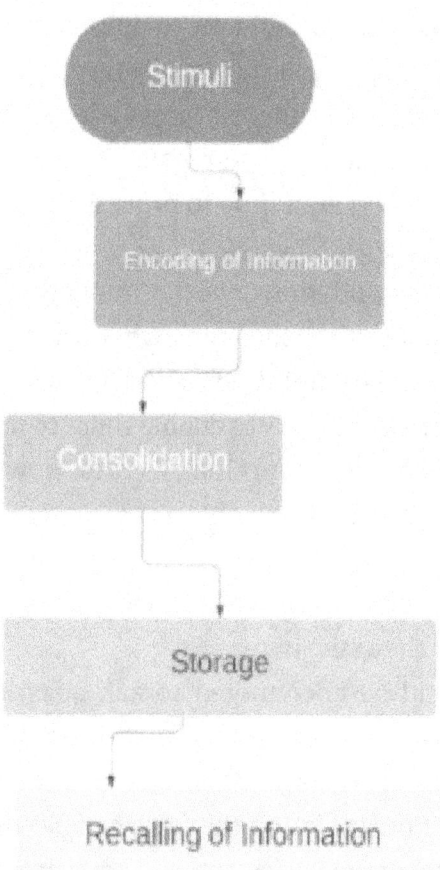

An hour-long lecture at school exposes a student's mind to a tonne of new knowledge, including names, concepts, facts, and other figures. They must provide their brains enough time to consolidate information obtained by them. They can make it a habit to write down all they learn and to provide an original summary.

It takes time for new knowledge to register in our minds. Our brains can only store information in short-term memory for brief periods of time. It can hold on to a maximum of seven characters at once. Looking at our children's school lives, we see that they are given little time to process a lot of information. It's a great deal more than we can recall. For this reason, we need to give ourselves enough time to process the information we are learning.

Giving time for consolidation does not imply that we should go find a solitary spot to sit. Rehearsing what you have heard or seen in your mind can be helpful. One strategy to help students retain material in their minds is to enable them to meditate for five minutes following each hour-long lecture. However, there are other methods as well, like:

- As soon as a student attends a lecture at school, it may be requested that they take notes.
- Students should be encouraged to ask questions of the teacher. It further aids in the consolidation of information.
- After taking notes in class, he or she should continue to go over them. Consolidating the facts can be considerably aided by going over them a few times. They can get a notepad meant just for taking notes.
- Taking notes on each paragraph after reading is another strategy that's quite popular with pupils. You have the option to take notes on the sides of the book they are reading or in a different notebook.
- He or she is able to form an internal mental picture of what they were taught in school. He or she can attempt to picture

what saffron looks like, how it is cleaned and separated from the plant, and how it is used in meals and the process of manufacturing various medicines if they are learning about saffron and its benefits as a herb in meals (Memory Principles, n.d).

Tricks to Remember Information?
I've discussed the idea that even though our brains have infinite storage, occasionally we forget things. There are instances when we store information in our brains but are unable to retrieve it later on. Our recollections fail us. There are moments when recall is not only challenging but also impossible, which can cause disappointment and frustration. Consider the scenario where a student starts writing a question during

an exam and then forgets the keyword. For students, recall is crucial. You can teach your child these memory-boosting techniques if they're not doing well in school. There are a few easy ways to improve your memory.**Convert Words into Images**

The goal for students should be to translate words into images. Because our brains receive visual information more efficiently than spoken information, this is an excellent workout.

Second, through the process of turning words into images, students can utilize

employing multiple senses to comprehend a lesson.

A student, for instance, had a presentation the other day. She can mentally establish a mental reminder to begin working on her presentation preparation for tomorrow evening by seeing a projector, a computer, and a pile of notes. Your brain stores information more effectively and reduces the likelihood of forgetting things when the picture is more vivid.

Memory Spots

The first strategy is linked to the formation of memory locations within your brain. You can consider the actual areas in your life that you want to be in, like the TV lounge, automobile, or kitchen. Place the image you've learned to make in

the first trick in that particular area of your mind. Referring back to the earlier example, the student is able to see her presentation as well as the TV lounge where her preferred television program is shown. She can see her presentation playing on the television in her mind's image. Similar memory locations can be formed in students' brains for both homework and lecture material. I used to match physics principles and formulas with the electronic devices my father got me while I was a student.

Don't Forget to Stack

We've talked about using an image to create a single memory location, but on a daily basis, we need to store a lot more data. With the aid of this process, we can add more details. A student may, for instance, place a pile of books next to the television where the presentation was being shown. She can connect the study materials she needs to look over in order to get ready for the presentation to that stack of books. She can then enhance the picture with a stack of vibrant papers. The colors she wishes to use to fill the pages of her presentation can be related to those stacks of papers. We assisted the learner in effectively stacking three memory locations in her brain. You can continue accumulating, and you can add as many memory locations as you are able to handle.

To ensure that the pictures stay together when stacked, try to make them as vibrant as possible. Therefore, your pupil should focus on creating vivid visuals if they wish to retain information accurately.

Study in the Afternoon

Most people think that studying in the morning, or doing any kind of learning activity, improves memory. Our brains are fresh after a long night, so anything we learn in the morning stays with us for a long time slumber. Despite common assumption, studying in the afternoon aids in memory retention. Research indicates that studying in the afternoon is beneficial because it sets us up for a restful sleep cycle, and after studying, we tend to retain information better. This raises the issue of what would happen if we went to bed after studying in the morning. Our brains will function similarly, but since most individuals don't go to bed in the morning, afternoon study is the most effective and strongly advised that students.

Role of Emotions in Memory

Experts, scholars, and medical professionals have disagreed on the importance of emotions in memory formation. Answering the question is not as straightforward and easy as it looks. Humans have feelings that are multifaceted, which makes it challenging to comprehend how they relate to memory functions. This topic has two branches: the first deals with the emotional content of the information that students are receiving, and the other with the students' emotional states.

People are well known to remember emotionally charged information. Events and facts that are uninteresting and abstract have a hard time sticking in their recollections. How long a memory stays in our brain depends on how strong the emotions are at the time. The significance of an event has little bearing on whether it becomes a memory or not. I once went to the hospital as a child with my uncle to see people who had been in auto accidents. I had no need to visit the hospital, and I didn't know them. When my uncle learned about the accident, I was in the market with him, so I had to accompany him as he hurried to the trauma center. Because of the horror I had when I saw them covered in blood, the recollection is as vivid as it was the day it happened. The feelings I went through when viewing them in the hospital are still present in me. The feelings were so intense that I lost consciousness for a brief period of time before regaining consciousness. My memory was permanently affected by the occurrence (The Role of Emotion in Memory, n.d).

We might sacrifice other information to store intense emotional impressions in our memory. This implies that a student is unlikely to recall anything they learnt in class before to the event if they are returning from school having absorbed a ton of new material and they encounter something that is really emotional.

Events that are emotionally charged eclipse the knowledge that has already been collected but is still in its infancy and transitory stage in our working memory. I can't remember why I was with my uncle that day, or why we were in the market doing what we were doing. All I can recall is what I witnessed at the hospital. Women are more susceptible to this emotional influence than men are (The role of emotion in memory, n.d.).

Depending on which memories are connected to happy or negative feelings, our brain processes them in a different way. The age of a pupil and other variables appear to have an impact on this rule. The primary distinction between happy and bad memories is that pleasant memories are easier for our brains to forget than unpleasant ones. This is true for youth as well. Individuals experiencing mild depression equally forget both types of memories. Older people are better able to control how much information they retain and how much they discard. Their emotional regulation is stronger. In order to prevent despair, kids gradually teach themselves to encode less when they encounter a difficult circumstance.

According to studies, pleasant memories have more sensory information than bad ones. Emotionally charged events in our life stick with us for a very long time. Positive memories are more vividly pictured in our brains than bad ones. Contextual information that help develop a better recall are abundant in positive recollections. Emotional power shapes memory development.

Emotional State of Mind

This represents the second scenario I mentioned. The imprinting process in our brains will be impacted if we are experiencing an emotional mental state and the sight we are observing is emotionally neutral. Our memory is influenced by our mood.

Whether we are joyful, depressed, furious, or dissatisfied affects what we see, hear, and encode. For instance, our brain will only receive bad memories when we are depressed. Maybe that is why depressing music is so popular. Individuals enjoy listening to it while they're feeling down and discouraged.

There's another method to link the mood with the event. When our attitude at the time of information retrieval corresponds with the mood when The recollection was something we made. Additionally, we may recall events and data more readily in this fashion. Our memory is also impacted by how we respond to particular events or facts. The control we exercise over our responses to specific emotional experiences influences our memory. My recall of the occurrence at the trauma center is easily traceable because of my outstanding and remarkable response to it. I fled the medical department as soon as I saw the victims were badly bruised and covered in blood, passing out on the floor. A few seconds of unconsciousness followed, but the response was so strong that the memory endured (The Role of Emotion in Memory, n.d).

In our lives, we experience a number of intensely emotional experiences that fail to elicit a strong response from us. For this reason, they finally vanish into thin air, leaving no trace in the depths of our history.

Because of this, we are unable to remember intensely felt events, despite the efforts of friends and family to convince us that they happened. The emotional experience I had raises the question of whether worry or the severity of a bad incident is what helps us remember things better. If this is the case, then the theory that stressful situations and depressive and anxious feelings sharpen our memories ought to hold water as well. That's not quite the whole story, we know. Research indicates that only mild anxiety can enhance our memory without negatively impacting the functioning of other memory-related areas. Similar to this, happiness influences some types of performances in a favorable way while interfering with others. Let's examine the ways in which distinct emotions impact various brain regions.

When we witness or experience anything, the emotions we are feeling are important. We retain information longer when we are experiencing stronger emotions.

Despite what the general public believes, we have the ability to control how much or how little we express our emotions when we see an incident or discover new information. A pupil can evoke strong feelings of delight and curiosity when they encounter images of a specific flower, plant, or tree. These feelings will assist him or her in remembering the details related to them. They are able to practice evoking strong feelings more than once. They can also turn this into a method for improving their ability to recall new information. All they have to do is program their brain to respond to novel information in a specific way.

Information presentation is equally significant. When she is learning something new, she ought to wear it on her face and incorporate it into her movements (The Role of Emotion in Memory, n.d).

The Connection Between Emotion and Attention

Various research indicates that there is a functional relationship between our attention and emotional inputs. As they go through the brain in parallel streams, they really merge together in a specific area of the brain known as the frontal cingulate. We pay greater attention to emotionally charged events than to anything else because of this. For this reason, when pupils are curious about a subject or topic, they learn more effectively. When we are aroused emotionally, we are not really distracted.

Our brain keeps itself in a condition of preparedness to respond when we react emotionally to a circumstance. Maintaining a system that establishes our threshold for how we ought to react to an outside stimulus is another benefit it provides.

One way to think of attention is as a type of mental activity that is brought on by heightened emotions. In actuality, these arousals modify it.

Cortisol, a stress hormone produced by our body, interacts with the amygdala. The other areas of our brains' activity can be changed by the amygdala, which we can control. Influencing the consolidation process is the most common way it modifies our brains (The Role of Emotion in Memory, n.d).

How Emotional Arousal Help Students in Learning New Things

It is a known fact that emotions have a good impact on memory when it comes to recalling details. It is not that hard to integrate emotional experiences into a school setting. Should a student engage in combat when they are with someone, they are not likely to focus on the lessons being taught. They need to let go of their anger before they can begin to learn. They are unlikely to replace their rage with curiosity if they are unable to express it. In order to suppress or manage their emotions, students can learn how to take charge of their rational thought processes. This is important because when we are upset about anything, all we can think back on is that one instance which became the source of our rage, and that specific incident replaces all that comes after it. Instructors might start a class activity that relieves tension, such singing or telling a joke. Teachers can also challenge their students' emotional states by incorporating their own emotional experiences into what they are trying to teach them.

Attention

Working memory and attention are closely related in the brain. Both are thought to be essential for learning and daily life. These are two facets of executive functioning that facilitate the intake and reception of new information gathered from our environment. Contrary to popular belief, the two are not the same thing. Let us examine their nature and impact on the memory process.

What Is Attention?

It is believed that the process of paying attention enables us to take in new information. Furthermore, it facilitates the process of choosing from among the information that we consistently receive. Focus is comparable to a

funnel via which we can filter out information we'd prefer to lose and choose what to keep in our minds. For instance, a student who excels in English literary classes may struggle in medicine classes because she pays more attention in English literature lectures than in medical lectures. When learning something new, a student needs to be mindful of several aspects of attention.

- Being vigilant is the first factor. Pupils must to be prepared to pay close attention in class. If They are unlikely to gather their thoughts and direct them toward their lecturers' lectures if they allow them to stray from the whiteboard or book to PlayStations.
- The second aspect is that pupils need to learn how to decide what is and isn't worthy of their attention. They have to be able to decide what is worthy of their focus. For instance, they

ought to concentrate on what the instructor is saying and ignore the other conversations in the hallway. The ability of students to maintain focus for a predetermined amount of time is the third thing to take into account. Students suffer when given an endless amount of time to stay attentive since they will get tired quickly. Instructors ought to be specific. the duration of the lecture, such as five, ten, or thirty minutes.

● Teachers should ask pupils to focus on the new knowledge as it is introduced, whenever it becomes necessary during the lesson. Concerning attention management, classrooms play a critical role. Instructors must constantly adjust their pupils' attention spans to match the content being presented. A pupil with attention problems won't be able to remember key points from the lesson.

What Is Memory?

A student's bucket of short-term memory receives the fresh feed once they have gathered information through attentive listening. It remains there for a while till the encoding procedure is completed. Our brain evaluates the information it has been given and modifies it to be helpful for our upcoming endeavors. Working memory is the mechanism by which the information is appropriately processed in the short-term memory.

Additionally, working memory is a quick process. Before being transferred to long-term memory, information only remains there for a brief period of time. When we are engaged in another activity, working memory enables us to take in new information. Some pupils express dissatisfaction at their inability to recall the meaning. of basic adjectives and words, whereas others are able to recall and remember them with ease. The way a

CHAPTER 4. METHODS AND SYSTEMS OF REMEMBERING INFORMATION

student's brain processes information is the source of the issue. For instance, an English language instructor might be teaching her students about adjectives like slick, bright, slow, fuzzy, or confused. A pupil will not be able to store new information in their memory to be recalled later if they are unable to process it in their brain.

Students can use their working memory to process this information by associating each adjective with an entity in their minds. If they are unable to think of anyone else, they can connect all of them to either themselves or their teacher. By doing this, students are breaking down new material into smaller chunks that are then stored in long-term memory. Above all, what matters most to a person is the information's significance and applicability.

Students have effectively retained a large amount of material in their long-term memory by the end of the lecture. When the teacher asks them to respond to a question regarding what they had read a short while earlier, we may access and recall specific knowledge from this location. A student will struggle to store information into long-term memory if they are not paying attention to what they are learning throughout the lecture. This is because they won't be able to process it in working memory. Thus, we can link our attention to long-term memory and knowledge retrieval if we turn back time and turn our brain back to the beginning of the subject. Information retrieval will suffer if we are not paying close attention.

There are several stages in the memory process for working memory and attention. When it comes to learning, they are both crucial. As we all know, children who struggle with attention also struggle with remembering. Problems with attention eventually result in problems with the learning process (Rosen, n.d.).

Imagination

Imagined things are not the same as remembered ones. What we perceive through hearing, seeing, and touching becomes a memory. However, imagination is based on what we have experienced. When we visualize something, it feels in our minds just as real as an actual event or observable memory.

The term "imagination" describes a person's creative ability. We've all heard that a particular painter or director of films is innovative and creative. When describing a work of art, we frequently use terms like "Great imagination." There is another meaning for the word imagination, which is mental imagery of any kind. I can bring my house back to the way it was before various renovations were made. A Mental images are constructs we make up in our minds. Singing along to a song and attempting to remember the words is another way to use our imagination.

Humans have a special capacity for imagination. It enables people to search for novel concepts that are absent from their current surroundings. To put it plainly, imagination is all about the fantastical. We are able to picture someone we recently met. In a similar vein, we can envision a state-of-the-art aircraft that does not exist. Science fiction is created in this manner.

Novelists and filmmakers create fantastical worlds with their vivid imaginations. Memory and imagination are related in that memory is used by imagination to conjure up specific mental images. As You already remember seeing an airplane when you see the image of one. Simply use your imagination to add a few more aspects to the airplane, and you'll be able to create a whole new mental image.

It's similar to a virtual reality program where our imagination conjures up imaginary images. This, according to experts, explains why we dream clearly. Using our imagination, our minds conjure up pictures that we view when we sleep.

Memorizing Verbatim Text

Memorization is not as difficult as most people think. The issue is that we have limited memory to the task of spinning a wheel—that is, repeating information over and over. Maybe our strategy isn't the best one after all. To be able to memorize, we still have a lot to learn. The human brain is better at recalling stories and concepts than it is at memorizing exact objects and text word for word. Are recitation and repetition the only two ways to learn something by heart?

Or are there other ways to accomplish that in place? Fortunately, there are additional techniques we may employ to teach our brains to efficiently memorize information.

When we are reading a book we wish to memorize; it causes certain brain regions to fire. Rather to just repeating or reciting what we have learnt, we should concentrate on remembering it. One math student, for instance, studied two times tables in class. Rather than repeating the tables by looking at a book, the best method is to read them aloud and then mentally refresh your memory.

Take a few minutes to memorize a passage from a speech. So that we may easily recollect the speech in our minds, we must memorize it. Let's examine a few strategies that may help us memorize information more effectively.

- The first approach is to read the speech passage aloud enough for you to Listen to it with your ears.
- Writing the text down, word by word, in a notebook is the second stage.
- Reading the entire text from the notepad and making a broad outline is the third step. Every point in the plan should allude to a concept in the speech.
- Talking to someone else who can read the text aloud to you is the fourth stage.

5

CHAPTER 5. SUPER MEMORY TRAINERS

Mnemonics are an efficient method of learning new information and retaining it in your mind for a long time. Its goal is to reduce the amount of time your brain needs to absorb abstract concepts such as mathematical tables, formulas, diagrams, and other things. By connecting new information to previously acquired knowledge, mnemonics help speed up the encoding of data in the brain.

You will learn how to make mnemonics for numbers, dates, faces, and difficult words from the SAT vocabulary in this chapter. You will also learn how to make mnemonics to help you memorize lists when you need to run to the grocery store or fruit stand.

They are called "ultimate memory enhancers." With the help of mnemonics, we can train our memory to become a super memory that can effectively process information of any type and size.

Mnemonics 1: Remember Words Not Related to Each Other

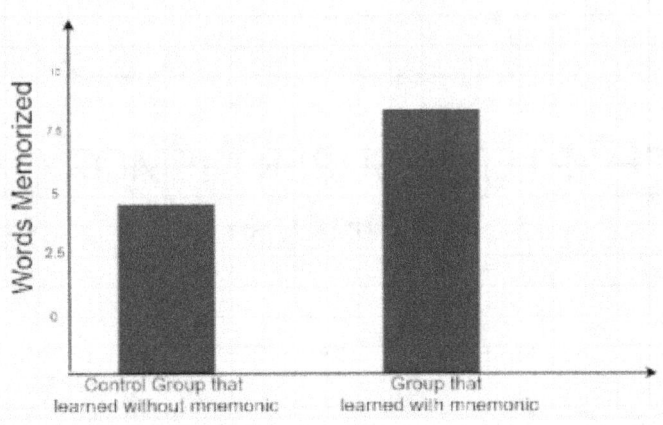

It can be difficult to commit new words to memory. Nobody is capable of doing this feat. Using mnemonic devices can help you learn and retain words at an extremely fast rate. I'm going to talk about a two-pronged strategy. It centers on whether a term contains stressed syllables. How we may memorize information using stressed syllables seems to be a little enigmatic. Our brain is predisposed to stressed syllable sounds for unexplained reasons. We are more likely to recall a word for a longer period of time if the sound is distinct.

Unstressed syllables, on the other hand, find their proper position in our brains without seeking particular attention from our brains.

Instead of wasting time on unstressed syllables in words, students should concentrate on the stressed syllables. They can learn a greater variety of vocabulary more quickly this way, saving them more time. Now let's learn some mnemonics to help you remember specific terms. Making a customized mnemonic is the most effective method for learning a new word. An image or a brief narrative related to the definition of the term might be used to help build the mnemonic.

Because our brains are naturally predisposed to remember uncommon information, the mnemonic should be strange and unexpected. You can use an image to assist you use the term more frequently, particularly when you see something that corresponds with the picture in your head or something that brings up the definition of that word. In both situations, the original word appears in front of you, making it easier for you to picture. This closes the semantic gap between the word and its meaning. Once the word has become ingrained in your memory, you are no longer required to recall the mnemonic. An English word's mnemonic is as follows:

Word References to Mnemonic Points

The result

This is an illustration of a term in the English language.

Keep in mind that the stressed syllable of the word you are focusing on should serve as the foundation for your mnemonic.

● The mnemonic for the word wearisome is wearisome. Include an illustration that alludes to the term "wear," like putting on clothes after a chilly dip in a frozen lake or wearing a tea shirt in the heart of a shopping center. You will be able to remember the term for the rest of your life if the syllable is stressed and the visual is strange. This is because the word and its meaning will undoubtedly spring to mind every time you see, hear, or see someone wear the word.

● The word appear, which will cause the mnemonic to emerge, is the second example. Include a picture of a pear that you've eaten or that you've seen dangling from a tree. Make an effort to link the term with the image. as well as its significance. Try using your imagination to conjure up a strange image if you can't recall one from your memory. You could visualize yourself, for instance, plucking pears from a garden or jungle tree. Maybe you fell gently while removing it from the tree, or maybe the gardener noticed you and chased after you while holding a stick. This can help you to recall the definition of the word "appear" and its meaning the next time you see a pear, wherever you may be. The gap will eventually close, and you won't require the image any more.

At that point, you can erase the mnemonic from your mind.

● Topple is the third word. On the stressed syllable, the mnemonic should be placed. Topple is the result. Try now to associate the term "top" with an image, such an eagle you spotted having lunch atop a hill. You hurt your ankle trying to get close to him, and you failed. One more unusual picture could be of an eagle perched atop your business tower. As you attempt to take a picture of him, he assaults you, pulling your hair and almost knocking you over the building. You can link the word's meaning and the visual in this way.

● The term brace serves as the fourth example. This example can be used to construct two different kinds of mnemonics: brace and Put on a brace. The first is preferable since it is simpler to recall and is based on a widely used word. Include a picture of a horse race at a stadium. The horses are galloping toward the finish line. The black horse on whom you have wagered unexpectedly stumbles and strains his front leg. In order to provide the horse with a brace and alleviate his agony, you dash to the doctor. You can recall the word and its meaning if you associate the image with the word brace. Once the word has effectively taken up residence in your mind, the visual will eventually fade from memory.

Mnemonics 2: Remember Complex Words

As a high school student preparing for the SAT, you have a lot of difficult English vocabulary to commit to memory. The English language has an enormous vocabulary with many multisyllable words that tax our mental capacity. They can retain the words for a brief period of time if they repeat or recite them in order to memorize them. They must come up with mnemonics for every word they read if they hope to retain them for a longer period of time. Mnemonics are frowned upon by many pupils since they take time to learn. However, the reality remains that it is the sole strategy that aids in our long-term memory retention. Among mnemonics are similar to tools that aid with memory. Mnemonics for difficult words might be patterns of letters, images, or concepts. Anything that you can recall can be it. Let's examine a few instances.

Let us consider the word adversity as an example.

● A state of misfortune and affliction is called adversity.

This is how we may deconstruct the word: ad-ver-sity. Ad stands for city advertisements. Sity is the noun form of city. We can associate certain word segments with various things in this way.

The connotation is related to the unfortunate situation of low-income individuals who perform menial employment in industry.

● The word friendly comes next. The adjective "amicable" connotes friendliness and good intentions. The The word's mnemonic will be friendly and amiable. Mic is the abbreviation for microphone, and it is typically wired. You can recall the term amiable in this way. Include a picture of someone complimenting their friends and family while speaking into a microphone.

You can retain the word and its meaning in this way. You are free to disregard the visual after the word has cemented itself firmly in your memory.

- The word "capitulate," which denotes living in a situation within predetermined guidelines, serves as the third example. Capital and late will serve as the acronym for the phrase "capitulate." Take note of the bolded words: surrender.

While the other word is only in half form, one word is in its whole form. People arrive late every time. in a nation's capital due to traffic jams and an overwhelming volume of traffic. In this way, you can link a complex term to a previously learned basic word. You can attach these lines to a picture of a factory worker sprinting across a subway platform to catch a train if you'd want to add some visuals. He can't miss the one who is about to leave the station because he is already running late for work.

- Another difficult word is compassion. This word expresses a profound sympathy for the plight of others. Compass and passion should be the word's mnemonic. Imagine an individual who enjoys gathering compasses and presenting them as presents. to underprivileged kids out of kindness. We can better recall the word's meaning with the aid of this image.

These techniques are really easy, particularly after we get the hang of making mnemonics. It's evident how basic they are. Learning with mnemonics mastery is how students should learn. This will expand their vocabulary and improve their brain's capacity for quick recall in addition to helping them retain more words.

Additionally, we can learn difficult foreign words by heart with the aid of basic mnemonic devices. I'll be making a mnemonic with a few Spanish words.

● Having knowledge about ● porke ● oatro

The following shows how the terms listed above relate to words in the English language.

● Having knowledge about ● porke ● oatro It is now much simpler to remember thanks to us. Every time you see a word in bold, you will be able to recall the whole word. This method improves the process of learning foreign language. You can give each word a different visual to increase the effectiveness of the mnemonic exercise.

The picture might show the terms you highlighted within an unfamiliar word. For instance, I have highlighted the word "bear" in the first word. You can associate the Spanish term with the mental picture of a bear (Vocabulary: How to memorize vocabulary faster than ever, n.d.).

Mnemonic 3: Remember the Numbers

What could be more challenging to retain than intricate vocabulary? The numbers are what matter. The general public believes that numbers are the most powerful, even though they are the easiest to learn challenging to recall. Experts attribute our brain's incapacity to retain numerical values. They contend that most individuals forget numbers but recall locations, narratives, and images because our brains lack the inherent substance needed to retain numbers. Let's look at a number and see whether we can recall it with ease. This is the phone number:

3830568856659

Can you commit it to memory all at once? Give it another go. Could you finish it now? You are not the only one. Most people have difficulty remembering things. data that is displayed as a numerical format. You will be able to recite it by recalling it from memory for a little period of time if you just keep repeating it for about twenty minutes. After a day or two, or after some time, you will undoubtedly forget it. Check the following number now:

38305, 6885, 6659

Learning has undoubtedly been more easier. We can quickly and effectively memorize information by breaking it up into multiple sets. By putting the three components into words, such sixty-eight eight-five and sixty-six fifty-nine, you can help yourself remember them.

Making abstract concepts into easily remembered symbols or images is the golden rule of memory retention. As an illustration, you can transform the numbers into pictures, which you can then input into a memory palace. Now let's look at building a memory castle. Attempt to construct a mental palace with a living area, main entrance, and backyard in your mind. There are so three places in the memory palace.

The first place is where the number 38305 can be entered. Since it is simpler to recall what occurs first in a sequence, the first number in a sequence can be larger than the others. Now is the time to see yourself standing in front of a house. On the

CHAPTER 5. SUPER MEMORY TRAINERS

porch in front of the front entrance, there is a postbox suspended from the ceiling.

The number 38205 should be inscribed in bold and italics on that post box. You want to know if the number was written by the home's owner for good fortune or if it refers to the quantity of bricks that were used to build the home.

The initial portion of the number has been correctly entered into its designated spot (How to memorize numbers (an intro), n.d.).

The second portion of the number, 6885, now takes the lead. There is a backyard in our home. Enter the residence by opening the door. Locate the path leading to the backyard. This allows us to place the four numbers in each of the backyard's four corners. Just one number keeps happening again. It can be placed in the corners facing one another. You can put the remaining two numbers in the remaining two corners. An arrow with six on the tail and five on the head should be positioned in the middle. This implies that six has had one digit removed in order to become five. The four numbers are strategically positioned in the backyard's four corners. Currently, you must write the entire number in the middle of the grass using the sand (How to memorize numbers (an intro), n.d.).

It's time to resolve the third component of the number now that the second part is likewise in the proper location. One location in our hypothetical The living room of the house is empty. Typically, couches, beds, and carpets are found in living rooms. A table is also provided for books to be read before bed. Sixty-six fifty-nine is the number's last portion. There are sixty-six books arranged on a tiny rack inside the space. The digital clock displayed the number fifty-nine just before it ceased functioning. In this approach, we can conjure up pictures in our minds and fill them with numbers to help us remember them more effectively. We refer to these kinds of mental residences as memory palaces.

You are correct if you believe that the workout takes a lot of time. Although it takes a lot of effort, it works incredibly well for remembering long formulas and ID numbers as well as payment card details. I've already described why chunking is the greatest method for memorizing short numbers (How to memorize numbers (an intro), n.d.).

Mnemonics 4: Remember Phrases and Passages

For most pupils, memorizing passages and phrases might be challenging. It is one of the more difficult intellectual tasks. You frequently find yourself unable to recite a passage of text when asked, even after you have studied it thoroughly.

Sometimes you can begin the recitation right away, but you end up stopping before you get to the end because you forget what you need to say. It is not possible to just resume where you left off (How to memorize passages, n.d.).

Memorizing the opening line of a passage or phrase is the most effective approach to letters. The piece or phrase may be a brief speech, a line from a book, or a communication from a friend. Consider the case of a young child who is now reciting an idiom that they have learned. You can keep track of the number of times he or she needs to be reminded to recite it all the way through. The most frequent issue that pupils face is that they simply forget the initial word of the sentence they have learned by heart. They are prompted to remember the complete sentence or section by the first word. Thus, if students develop the practice of coming up with their own prompts, they won't need to ask you for them in the future.

Let's quickly go over a few instances (How to commit quotes to memory, n.d.

● The saying "Beggars cannot be choosers" is colloquial. In the example, you can designate the two words as prompts. I want to use pickers and beggars as cues to remember the full sentence.

Another saying that comes to mind is "These red poppies are a dime a dozen." In this example, you can define other prompts, such red, dime, and dozen. Once you are proficient in mnemonics, you can place two prompts; nevertheless, a lengthy sentence needs to have three prompts at the beginning.

We now need to demonstrate how to use prompts to help memorize an example of a passage. I'll consider the Constitution's preamble as the US as an illustration.

We the People of the United States do ordain and establish this Constitution for the United States of America in order to form a more perfect Union, establish justice, ensure domestic tranquility, provide for the common defense, promote the general welfare, and secure the blessings of liberty to ourselves and our posterity.

The first sentence, "we the people of," is what you need to keep in mind. We need to provide several prompts because the text is lengthy in order for us to fully recall it. You can use the following phrases as prompts, for instance: To create a more perfect Union, uphold justice, ensure domestic peace, fund the common defense, advance the welfare of everyone, and ensure our own blessings from liberty

Another option is to make a term like PUJDTDWL out of the section above.

You can just learn the term by heart if you are unable to pronounce it. Thus, we possess a list of terms that we can utilize as cues to help us recall the entire paragraph. In the passage, I have the prompts set as nouns. It could seem a little strange and annoying to some kids. Instead, they may focus on the verbs. Here is how the prompts will be configured:

To secure the blessings of liberty to ourselves, create justice, ensure domestic tranquility, provide for the common defense, and form a more perfect union (How to memorize texts, n.d.).

Mnemonic 5: Remember Mixed Lists

Every household has to deal with groceries and other kitchen necessities on a regular basis. We must constantly bring them in from the market. The issue arises when we begin to misplace items while traveling. Writing things down and keeping them in our jacket pocket is the most effective method of helping us remember them. But occasionally, we misplace the written list. We can speak with our spouse over the phone, but can you just image how annoying it is to have to follow every word, buy the item, and then ask for the next one again? Why not practice some strategies for list memorization?

Typically, a list consists of a series of words and numbers. like a shopping list.

We can strengthen our memory for recalling lists by using some tried-and-true techniques and memory aids. We can condense a lengthy and tedious list into a short mnemonic. A list that might otherwise be boring can become memorable and catchy with the use of mnemonics.

We can utilize the first letter of each word on the list to successfully make a word mnemonic, after which we can create a new word or phrase. We can improve the list's memorability by doing this. Mnemonics can be used on any kind of list, not simply the grocery list—for example, the planets' positions in the solar system. or the mathematical operation sequence. Let's look at several mnemonic devices to help us remember information.

- A math student can memorize a list of mathematical operations by using mnemonic devices. Put eggs, muffins, donuts, and syrups in the kitchen, for instance. Information on parenthesis, exponents, multiplication, division, addition, and subtraction is contained in this statement.

● The expression mnemonic, which you can use to help you recall lists, is a fairly basic mnemonic. I plan to implement it on the list of planets around the sun. On a sheet of paper, we can create circles with a point in the middle that represents the sun. After that, we can write the planet names along with their suggested placements. Take Mercury, Venus, Earth, Mars, Jupiter, Uranus, and Neptune as an example. Pluto has been taken off the list of planets; astrologists now refer to it as a dwarf planet, thus I have deleted it.

●As with the mathematical processes, giving words to planet names and other unrelated sequences is another way to help you remember them. We can construct the phrase that follows for the planets' names: We were just served noodles by my very earnest mother (How to Memorize List, 2019).

Mnemonics 6: Remember the Names of People

It can be difficult to commit people's names to memory. It could be the fundamentals of memory. Relationship problems and feelings of humiliation arise when we are unable to recall someone's name. Forgetting names is common.

Regarding people's faces, and there are simple methods for us to recall them. See how we can accomplish it.

Initially, we will require a trigger that enables us to retrieve a person's entire name and face from our conscious recollection. If we can just recall the trigger, we can only devise a mnemonic and make it function. We've previously spoken about the trigger model. The person's visage serves as the trigger in this instance. You ought to grow the mnemonic in such a way that you instantly recall the person's name when you look at them.

It's important to observe which facial features stand out more than the others when looking at someone's visage. Select the

CHAPTER 5. SUPER MEMORY TRAINERS

features that catch your attention and that you can still recall when you look at the same person in the future. Whatever the trait is, it must be distinct enough to stick in your memory.

For instance, a person's right eyebrow bears a scar mark. It's easy to tell when you look at his or her face. The individual is distinguished from other people by this quality. The scar can be made into a prompt to keep their name in mind the next time you see them. You'll discover that remembering their name the following time is quite simple because not everyone has facial scars.

The next step is to commit the person's name to memory. The person you are meeting should have an emphasized syllable if they go by a western name like Michael. In this instance, it is evident that Mike is under stress. The stressed syllable in Elizabeth's name is liz. While it is challenging to recall the entire name, it is much simpler to recall the stressed words, like Mike or Liz.

It's evident that people base their nicknames on stressed syllables. All that's left to do is to associate a tangible thing with the emphasized syllable. We could, for instance, attach Mike to the microphone. The task is the same as the one we completed with words and numbers. To associate the name with a tangible object, we require a mental picture. We can only strengthen our memory when it comes to remembering faces and names in this way.

You can now link it to the individual you just saw. We have a face with an eyebrow scar, and his name is associated with the word "microphone." Connecting the two is the last and next stage. Imagine that the man with the scar on his face is speaking into a microphone while holding A massive assembly of jokers. Jokers give an interesting and enjoyable touch to the image that helps us remember things for a long time.

You may locate the trigger on the person's face whenever they appear in front of your eyes, and the whole image of them appears.

He's addressing a crowd now, holding a microphone. You can quickly recall his name when you see the microphone in your mind's eye. The entire activity resembles a domino effect. The remainder of the process begins when you pull the trigger and concludes with you being reminded of the person's name.

This is an excellent mnemonic to help you recall people's names and faces.

You can benefit from this exercise. when you're meeting new people and on your second meeting, you call them by name, shocking them. This is how you expand your social networks and make friends with total strangers. Let's update the procedures:

- Finding the most unusual feature on the person's face is the first phase.
- Tailor the stressed syllable to resemble a tangible object is the second.
- Linking an object to the person's face is the third step.

This method of coming up with mnemonics is enjoyable, simple, and a great approach to help people recall names. It could take a while and be difficult the first time, but with a few tries, you'll be able to do it in a matter of seconds.

6

CHAPTER 6. HOW TO USE MNEMONICS IN SCHOOL LESSONS

Mnemonics offer us the best strategy for students to learn their lessons effectively at school. Every student has different tastes and preferences when it comes to learning and memorizing different things. One student can be good at learning mathematics but bad at understanding and memorizing chemical formulas. Similarly, a student is good at memorizing names of countries but bad at remembering dates of independence of different countries.

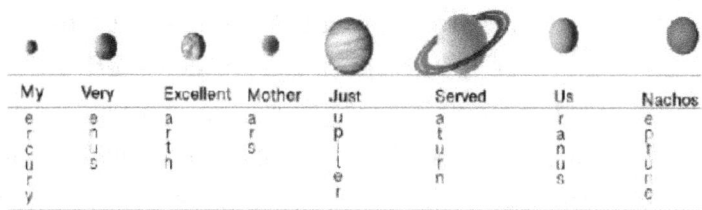

Using mnemonics can help you quickly retain abstract and

complicated knowledge on a variety of topics. This section will guide you through the process of making mnemonics to help you remember dates and activities. This is quite beneficial for history students. Making mnemonics to help with the memorization of mathematical formulas, tables, operators, physical equations, and chemical formulas is covered in one part. All of these concepts are too abstract to retain without the use of mnemonic devices.

It is doubtful that a student will retain the material in his head for very long, even if he is committed enough to practice and memorize the equations. There is a part in the chapter dedicated to learning the names of colors and flowers by heart. It concludes with the creation of mnemonics to help recall nation names.

Mnemonics for Dates and Events

Because they are so arbitrary and occasionally incredibly enigmatic unless we attempt to associate them with something particular, dates are thought to be the hardest things to remember. Allow me to transport you to the American Civil War commenced in 1861. Because there are so many dates to recall, we are unable to recall only the date. For instance, it is impossible to tally the number of dates and events in American history alone. The American Revolution, which began in 1783, is the starting point, and numerous other events that are worth talking about followed. Consider the American Civil War date, when the causes of slavery caused the North and the South to clash. If you instruct a pupil to commit only the date, chances are they won't remember it for a few days. You need to investigate what strange was going on on that day. Keep an eye out for anything that makes that day stand out from the others, such as a unique event or something else. For instance, I discussed how slavery and the American Civil War are related. You ought to explain to your pupil what makes 1861 unique in comparison to the other nineteenth-century years.

For history students, the mnemonic approach is quite helpful in this situation. A learner can learn many connections, patterns, and ideas with the use of a mnemonic system, which will help them retain and understand the material more easily. There are several There are many ways to accomplish it, but only the most effective ones are significant and beneficial to you. Generally speaking, the memorization process allows you to retain information using as many senses as possible (How to Remember Dates for a Test-Memorization, n.d.).

Simplify Things

The century in which the American Civil War occurred is already known to you if you are studying it in history class. Because the date needs to be made simpler, the first two digits of the year should be removed. In the first two numerals in the American Civil War case are 18. The date can be made simpler by reducing it to two digits, 61. This should make memorization simple and enjoyable.

You can divide the number into two pieces as well. According to How to Remember Dates for a Test-Memorization (n.d.), it is simpler to recall the numbers 18 and 61 than the entire 1861.

Mathematics

Using math to help you recall the dates is another strategy. You can apply addition, subtraction, multiplication, and division, among other mathematical operations. I'll continue using the illustration from the earlier part. The number 1861 is made up of the digits 18 and 61. Since one of the numbers is repeating, we have three to work with here. Let's create as many equations as we can using these three figures.

$8 - 1 = 7$.

$6 + 1 = 7$.

Since the answers to both equations are the same, it is simple to memorize.

Recall that there was no difference in the answers to the two equations. For the first equation, use addition; for the second, use subtraction (How to Recall Dates for an Exam-Memorization, n.d.).***Mental Images***

An additional often used technique is to display the number 1861 as a bar graph.

Four bars, each representing a single digit from the number, can be shown as a sort of bar graph. Construct the mental image and envision the American Civil War beside it as well. With muskets in hand, troops may be seen fighting in the second image. After that, you can merge the two pictures to create a link. You may then recall both the date and the linked event in addition to just the date itself.

In a similar vein, you can visualize a bar chart in your head and then place the image in the same memory location where you have insert a picture of the actual American Revolution. You can also create a mental narrative. You can write the story more easily if you use mental imagery. The likelihood that a narrative will stick in your mind increases with its level of humor and weirdness. To help you recall dates and events, you can make up a story based on the historical event's background. If you wish to commit a large number of dates to memory, this method can be useful. The smallest details regarding the historical event you wish to commit to memory must be considered. One popular method for learning historical events by heart is contextualization (How to Remember Dates for a Test-Memorization, n.d).

Before the American Civil War of 1861, there had a rich history. Before it began, the American Civil War of 1861 had a complicated history.

The war was ingrained in American society and culture. Numerous things happened that eventually caused two factions of society to start a civil war. You can get brief summaries of the reasons for the American Civil War and the occasions leading up to its outbreak on the internet. You can also look through pictures related to the American Civil War to help you retain the information effectively and for a long time. That is how you can conjure up a mental short tale about the American Civil War. That is your tale, and you will always remember it for some time (How to Recall Dates for Test Memory, n.d).

Mathematical, Physical, Chemical Formulas

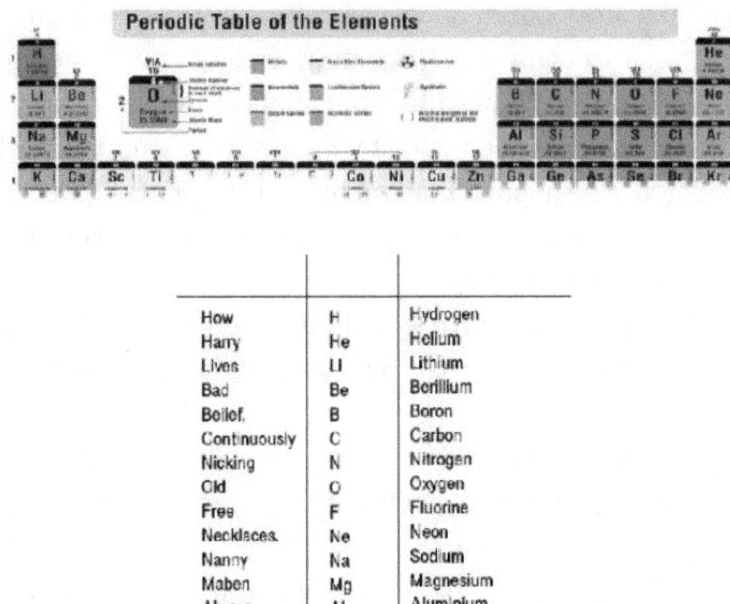

How	H	Hydrogen
Harry	He	Helium
Lives	Li	Lithium
Bad	Be	Berillium
Belief.	B	Boron
Continuously	C	Carbon
Nicking	N	Nitrogen
Old	O	Oxygen
Free	F	Fluorine
Necklaces.	Ne	Neon
Nanny	Na	Sodium
Maben	Mg	Magnesium
Always	Al	Aluminium

When it comes to learning really abstract concepts like periodic tables and chemistry formulas, mnemonic devices are fantastic. You can write a song on the periodic table and then commit the lyrics to memory. Now let's view the musical piece.

● Harry's Misguided Belief: Always nicking his old, free necklaces. Nanny Maben never moves, sees everything clearly, and is aware of all the dangers that very criminal men face. Companions Unite at Night.

Adorable Zen gardens face serious attacks. Brothers Karamazov Rob Young Sane. Zorro Takes Out More Tacky Junk. Ron Peterson Augments Caddying Income Smashing Shimlan Terriers. I scan the cashiers' badges.

● Vibrant Cissy Reads Numy's Poetry Death, homophobia, and timid yobbos are the god-fearing taboos that Liz Herminone tampered with with the red oscilloscope. Author Harry Tells

People Big Porkies At Red French, Irritated Palmist

- In actuality, The Party Puked Amply, Upsetting Nippers. Emily's friends made none while Caddy baked the cake.
- Lady Raffele Daubs's Advice: See His Arithmetic, Daring Rogue Wise. Clever, conceited Whippet Delights in Sad Woman (Music: The Periodic Table of Elements, undated).

This served as the periodic table's 18 element mnemonic. The lyrics, the melody, and the rhyme can all be altered. The word "How," which appears first in the table above, stands for helium. Using the initial letters of the elements in the periodic table, you can also create sentences and other words. After that, you can group the words and keep in mind each word's meaning inside the group (Song: Periodic Table of Elements, n.d.).

Among the most Memorization of dull and complicated material can be challenging. There are numerous chemical formulas and equations that need to be learned and retained. There are truckloads of items that need to be the nourishment for our memory. We couldn't possibly process such a vast amount of information without the aid of mnemonic devices. This adds enjoyment to the learning process.

The Orbitals

The orbitals are the first speed bump on our path to memorization of chemical formulas and pictures. Simply put, they are too complex for simple-minded individuals to understand. They are s, p, d, f, g, h, i, and k. It's a difficult order if not For pupils who are unfamiliar with chemistry, it is tough to recall. Now let's make our orbitals mnemonic. Take a look at this sentence:

Astute Law Enforcement Avoid Fishing Goldeye Hiding in the Kinnickinnic River

Properties of Elements

We are able to devise mnemonic devices for the various

elemental series. Examine the current metal series listed below.

Aluminum > Magnesium > Calcium > Sodium > Potassium > (Carbon)* > Zinc > Lead > Iron > Copper > Silver > Gold > Lead > Hydrogen

It is possible to rearrange this sequence to construct a sentence. Now let's examine the following:

Peter Quit Referring To Me As A Cute Zebra. Harry I Love You, Sober Goat

Here, I've utilized carbon, a non-metal, as a baseline (Prateek, 2017).

Mnemonics for Math

Mnemonic		
Please	P	Paranthesis
Excuse	E	Exponent
Me	M	Multiplication
David	D	Division
Adam	A	Addition
Sam	S	Subtraction

Math can be learned and memorized with the aid of mnemonics. Using the keyword strategy, which allows you to connect new, relevant knowledge to the keywords that represent mathematical equations and formulae, is the first method for memorization.

CHAPTER 6. HOW TO USE MNEMONICS IN SCHOOL LESSONS

You are already aware of this. When instructing in a classroom, you might utilize keywords that the pupils are already familiar with. The most effective technique to teach some multiplication facts is through keyword strategy. The most effective method is to associate each keyword with a mental image before committing it to memory. Here are a few of the most often used methods for teaching students how to memorize mathematical formulas and techniques (Using Mnemonic Instruction to Teach Math, n.d.).

The two families' visual representations ought to resemble the following:

- Two by two can be associated with the picture of an automobile's four wheels.
- The picture of six packs of Coca-Cola cans is related to 3 x 2.
- 4 x 2 is comparable to the picture of a spider with eight legs.
- The image of ten fingers or ten and toes can be associated with 5 x 2.
- The picture of a dozen oranges is related to 6 x 2.
- The picture of two weeks in a month can be associated with 7 x 2.
- 8 x 2 when added together can be associated with the picture of two spiders with 16 legs.
- An 18-wheeler dump truck image can be linked to 9 x 2.
- 10 x 2 is equivalent to the combined image of a human finger and toe.
- 11 x 2 is associated with the picture of a trailer with 22 wheels that is used to move containers.
- A picture of two dozen oranges is associated with the number 12 x 2.

The list can be expanded in this way to your desired length (Using Mnemonic Instruction to Teach Math, n.d.).

The pegword method is the second method for learning mathematical formulas and equations by heart. This particular technique represents numbers with a collection of rhymes. The rhymes, sometimes known as "pegwords," offer some graphic representations that correspond to mathematical facts. In this way, students can quickly acquire significant but dull facts and equations. This method is effective in teaching various branches of mathematics. Teaching a pupil the pegword "oranges" to establish a connection with the word six is the first step in teaching them the mathematical function of 3 x 2 = 6. Let's look at the next pegword method for teaching arithmetic to students.

- Making a flashcard with orange symbols on it is the first step in teaching using the pegword approach.
- Now instruct pupils on how to learn math facts using the pegword technique.
- Show them the multiplication mathematical operator.
- After giving them examples of three and two oranges, show them the equation's result—six oranges on the flashcard.

The When it comes to learning mathematical functions, the two methodologies mentioned above have been shown to be effective (Using Mnemonic Instruction to Teach Math, n.d).

Physics mnemonics are likewise quite fascinating and captivating. Let's examine a few of them. The formula for determining an object's weight is given at the outset. The following is the formula:

Where's = Miss G; $W = m \times g$

Here, W stands for the object's weight, m for the object's mass, and g for the strength of the gravitational field (Physics Equations with Mnemonics Flashcards Preview, n.d).

The second illustration is the distance covered. The following

CHAPTER 6. HOW TO USE MNEMONICS IN SCHOOL LESSONS

is the equation:

= v x t à same = extremely subdued

The distance traveled is shown by the letter s in the equation above by an item, where t is time and v is its velocity, or the speed at which it moved (Physics Equations with Mnemonics Flashcards Preview, n.d.).

The formula for calculating completed work is the next example. The following is the equation:

Women = Flashed Strength à W = F x s

The aforementioned equation denotes the work an object does (W), the force acting on it (F), and the distance the object travels as a result of the force's action (s) (Physics Equations with Mnemonics Flashcards Preview, n.d.).

The resultant force equation follows.

Full = Fatty = F = m an à Apple

F stands for the resulting force, m for the object's mass, and a for the acceleration of the thing. The momentum equation is the final example we will use. Let's look at the equation's mnemonics.

Zipper P = m v à pass = me

This equation (Physics Equations with Mnemonics Flashcards Preview, n.d.) uses the symbols p for momentum, m for mass, and v for the object's velocity.

Memorize Colors and Flowers

Most of the time, it's difficult to memorize the botanical names of flowers and other plants. For relatively basic names of flowers and other plants, botany uses some really difficult and esoteric terms. For instance, you can connect the
name of the flower From parasites to pets. Gazing can be transformed from gazania.

The most effective method for learning tough names is this kind of technique.

Let's look at some more plant names and see how to make mnemonics for them.

Papaver à paper (poppies)

Syringa (lilac) à Syringe Malus (apple) à Male

Let's discuss how to commit these mnemonics to memory. Make an effort to pronounce them clearly first, and then visualize the plant. If you haven't seen an image and are unable to visualize it, try searching on Google it or use a textbook to conduct some study. Find the word now, then add it to the picture. To help you remember it better, you can also mix two words and two images. I made a connection between syringa and the word syringe in the previous example. In order to remember it later, you can associate the pictures of the syringa and syringe in your mind's eye and keep them that way. The greatest way to retain information for a longer period of time is to use this technique (How to Remember Botanical Names, n.d).

Color mnemonics can be accommodated by our memory system. To help us remember colors and numbers better, we can associate visuals with them. Some folks simply don't understand why they are unable to recall the hues found in a rainbow.

Nonetheless, there are a few quick and simple memory techniques that might assist you in quickly and easily learning every hue in the globe. You may find it easier to learn and retain colors by using mnemonic techniques. Additionally, when you're feeling upbeat and energized, you can try to commit some hues to memory.

Consider the rainbow as an example. The following technique can be used to make a mnemonic to help you recall the colors in a rainbow. Make an attempt to construct a statement where the initial letters of each sentence encompass every color found in the rainbow.

Seldom Provided Delicious Soft, gummy ice cream Velaria

I've already described my favorite delicious ice cream in this sentence due of its distinct flavor and gummy texture. In this way, you can add additional hues, like blue, purple, violet, and sea green, to make different sentences. One method of memorization is this. Try coming up with some fresh sentences. List new ideas by brainstorming the titles of your favorite books or authors, or just about anything you can think of.

Remember Countries

The challenge of learning abstract country and capital names by heart often faces students. There are mnemonic devices that help with memorization, such as those for country names. As people, we are in love objects that are lively and engaging as opposed to boring and flat. Using mnemonics can add interactivity and intrigue to otherwise uninteresting country names.

The process is creating a collection of nations and giving them the names you choose.

Superb - Switzerland

Germany's Green

Luxembourg - Leaves

Gorgeous Belgium

You can see that because they form a logical sequence that sticks in our memory, the words I came up with to help us recall country names are simpler to remember than the names themselves (Mnemonic Devices to Study the European Nations, n.d.)

Conclusion

Can you commit a whole book to memory? Although the question appears absurd, it is actually quite legitimate. A deck of cards, a thousand numbers, a hundred thousand sentences, and many other things can be committed to memory by one individual. For certain individuals This accomplishment seems extremely easy, yet it is actually very challenging. As we have observed while going through the examples in this book, mnemonics have a strong ability to stimulate human behavior. All of us aspire to achieve exceptionally well in school by learning complete text books by heart.

I once had to deal with an embarrassing exam failure at school. For me, the day was just disastrous. Simply put, I was unable to remember anything I had studied the night before the test. A few years later, I discovered that I wasn't the only one who went through these phases of forgetting things.

Numerous people and organizations have conducted studies on the value and efficacy of mnemonics. Their ability to simplify and enhance the enjoyment of learning and memorization is possibly their most intriguing feature.

Mnemonics are entertaining tools that can be used to help you remember facts, dates, events, faces, figures, patterns, word sequences, and a wide range of other information.

You may flawlessly recall the most difficult of facts if you practice in the proper manner for a considerable amount of time. Memory aids, or mnemonics, are tools designed to help us learn and retain abstract information better.

Many students lament that they are unable to study the equations and formulas for chemicals. They claim that it is difficult for them and beyond their mental capacity, yet this is typically untrue. They possess the same mental capacity as other pupils. Their memory doesn't help them with their learning abilities, which is the only issue. So, they will perform better in class if parents and teachers assist them in learning how to make mnemonics for abstract concepts like chemical formulas. Mnemonics pose a challenge to conventional learning methods like rote learning and repetition, potentially even replacing them.

Mnemonics present an opportunity for us to test and enhance our memory.

It turns out to be an effective memory aid.

Conventional memorization methods are out of date, boring, and ineffective nowadays.

This is the reason mnemonic device creation should be taught to kids. They will realize that this is the most enjoyable approach to learn new things after they have mastered it. They will be able to hold onto large chunks of information in their brains for extended periods of time, which will enhance their memory. We benefit from mnemonics in both our short- and long-term memory.

It influences our imagination as well. It is a crucial method for forming strong mental images. We have attempted to offer visual aids for memorization of various pieces of information in several cases throughout the book. Do you recall the number memorization exercise where we imagined a house with two parts as well as a main gate? Numerous more activities emphasized the value of forming mental pictures and linking them to abstract concepts. Mnemonics assist us to sharpen our imagination and conjure up fascinating images in this way. It is also a beneficial mental practice.

A fantastic method to remove rote learning from its position is to use mnemonics. Students can only embrace creativity and originality and abandon recitations and repeats with this approach. It functions similarly to a sensory stimulation and can make learning a new language enjoyable. We've learnt that by making specific English words out of their spellings, we can recall foreign terms. Mnemonics, according to experts, can be more beneficial and successful. for students whose verbal proficiency has increased.

It assists new students in a quick and effective way.

Our brains fire new information-transporting and long-term memory-storing neurons whenever we attempt to recall something new. We may simplify and enjoy the process by using mnemonics. Additionally, it enhances the general functioning of our brains and preserves their health.

Additionally, mnemonics foster our imagination, which improves our ability to recall new knowledge and makes us more capable of making decisions.

The purpose of this book is to provide you with the best methods for making mnemonics to enhance your study techniques. You now know about the various kinds of memory, including sensory memory, recollections that arise spontaneously, and others.

Additionally, you now know why you forget things and what may be done to strengthen your memory. Furthermore, you have acquired knowledge on the fundamental concepts of memory retention as well as the causes of forgetting things. I've even included a few tips to help you retain new information for a very long period.

You now understand how emotions can impact our memory and ability to learn. The book's next two chapters concentrated on the use of tried-and-true methods for making mnemonics to help memorize a variety of information, including names, faces, numbers, text passages, phrases, mixed lists, complicated terms, and foreign words. Furthermore, you discovered how to instruct pupils in creating mnemonic devices using historical dates and events.

names of nations, colors and flowers, mathematical formulas, the United States, and chemistry and physics equations.

By coming up with unique mnemonics for the subjects you teach in the classroom, you can absorb the tips and apply them to your own teaching. Additionally, you can motivate your pupils to master the art of mnemonic device creation.

WRITTEN BY
  JULIA BOURN
  THANK YOU
  THE END

www.ingramcontent.com/pod-product-compliance
Lightning Source LLC
LaVergne TN
LVHW012000070526
838202LV00054B/4980